100
GREAT SNACKS
& APPETIZERS

ORLA BRODERICK

PHOTOGRAPHS BY
ROBIN MATTHEWS

WEIDENFELD
& NICOLSON
LONDON

CONTENTS

INTRODUCTION

Let's face it, we all have snack-attacks every now and then, whether it's because we're in a hurry, had a large meal earlier in the day or just need something to keep us going for a couple of hours. How often have you had friends visit on the spur of the moment and wanted to offer them something to eat that doesn't take hours to prepare, or wanted to impress guests with a tantalising array of canapés? Well, this book provides all the answers.

Divided into five chapters, there is something here to suit every occasion. Inspired by the wealth of ingredients that are now readily available from all corners of the world, the recipes are full of interesting tastes and textures. And all of them are very easy for you to make at home. Most are finger food that you can just pick up and eat, without having to bother with knives and forks.

So now you can entertain friends in style, with a choice of exciting combinations and flavours. Use your imagination and put together a selection of the recipes under a common theme. For instance, choose dishes from the different chapters to make up a Chinese, Indian or Greek evening. The possibilities are endless...

The equipment required to prepare the recipes is very straightforward, and will be found in most domestic kitchens. The list of essentials includes a good food processor, a sharp cook's knife, a heavy-based frying pan, a grater, a citrus squeezer, a measuring jug, a sieve, scissors, a pastry brush, a rolling pin, different sized mixing bowls, a handful of wooden spoons and spatulas, and a selection of metal cutters.

A final point – eating between meals, or relying on a snack to take the place of a meal, is not a sin. This is a book for all of us who love good food but have busy, hectic lifestyles.

THE STORECUPBOARD

Many of the ingredients used in this book can be found in a well-stocked storecupboard. The list below may seem long, but if you're an enthusiastic cook you'll be amazed at how much you already have. When you're shopping, just add a couple of 'extras' to your basket to keep in the cupboard for a rainy day. Most things have quite a good shelf life. Do bear in mind, though, that use-by dates need to be observed, and that some foods, once opened, must be kept in the fridge.

A well-stocked storecupboard doesn't mean a cramped, poorly organised, over-stocked cupboard. With this you don't know what you have or where anything is, and when you do finally manage to pull something out it's likely to be well past its use-by date. So be sensible and make the most of the space available to you. For example, a sturdy rack on the wall near the cooker can provide room for oils, vinegars and the sauces and flavourings that you use regularly. In deciding where to keep your storecupboard ingredients, choose a spot that is well ventilated and out of direct sunlight. And ensure that there is a regular turnover of ingredients.

Remember that the list here is only a guide, and should be tailored to suit your own requirements.

LARGE BOTTLE OF OLIVE OIL

LARGE BOTTLE OF SUNFLOWER OIL

DRUM OF VEGETABLE OIL

BOTTLES OF WHITE AND RED WINE VINEGAR

SMALL BOTTLE OF BALSAMIC VINEGAR

CAN OF ENGLISH MUSTARD POWDER

JARS OF DIJON AND WHOLEGRAIN MUSTARD

BOTTLE OF WORCESTERSHIRE SAUCE

BOTTLE OF TABASCO SAUCE

BOTTLE OF SWEET CHILLI SAUCE

JARS OF GREEN AND RED PESTO SAUCE

BOTTLES OF LIGHT AND DARK SOY SAUCE

BOTTLE OF TOMATO KETCHUP

JAR OF PEANUT BUTTER

JAR OF CREAMED HORSERADISH

JAR OF TAPENADE

JARS OF BLACK AND GREEN OLIVES

BOTTLE OF MANGO CHUTNEY

PACKETS OF CAYENNE PEPPER AND PAPRIKA

PACKETS OF GROUND CUMIN, CORIANDER AND CHILLI POWDER

PACKET OF SMALL DRIED CHILLIES

PACKET OF MUSTARD SEEDS

SMALL PACKET OF SAFFRON STRANDS

SMALL DRUM OF HOT CURRY POWDER

JARS OF MILD OR MEDIUM AND HOT CURRY PASTE

JARS OF THAI RED AND GREEN CURRY PASTE

JAR OF CLEAR HONEY

CANS OF CHOPPED TOMATOES

TUBE OF TOMATO PURÉE

TUBE OR JAR OF SUN-DRIED TOMATO PASTE

JAR OF SUN-DRIED TOMATOES IN OIL

PACKETS OF LIGHT AND DARK MUSCOVADO SUGAR

PACKETS OF GRANULATED AND CASTER SUGAR

PACKET OF PLAIN FLOUR

SMALL CARTON OF BAKING POWDER

SMALL CARTON OF BICARBONATE OF SODA

BOX OF CORNFLOUR

PACKET OF DRIED BREADCRUMBS

PACKET OF DRIED READY-TO-EAT APRICOTS

PACKET OF CHINESE NOODLES

PACKET OF SESAME SEEDS

BAG OF TORTILLA CHIPS

PACKET OF POLENTA

PACKET OF BULGAR WHEAT

JAR OF PICKLED HERRING

JAR OF ARTICHOKE HEARTS

JAR OF MUSTARD RELISH

JAR OF REDCURRANT JELLY

CAN OF CHICKPEAS

CAN OF SWEET RED PEPPERS (PIMIENTOS)

CAN OF ANCHOVY FILLETS IN OIL

CAN OF TUNA IN BRINE

CAN OF COCONUT MILK

BLOCK OF CREAMED COCONUT

PACKET OF VINE LEAVES IN BRINE

THE BASICS

IN THE REFRIGERATOR

The cook's life is made much easier if the following essentials are always on hand in the refrigerator. Most of these foods will keep well if stored in the correct conditions. For example, wrap cheese individually in greaseproof paper or foil and, after each use, put on fresh wrapping for further storage. Because eggs absorb odours very easily, keep them away from any strong-smelling foods in the fridge, and store them pointed end downward, in their box.

Try to buy unwaxed or organic citrus fruits, particularly if you are going to use the rind, and keep them in the salad compartment at the bottom of your fridge, along with the vegetables. (If you can only get waxed citrus fruits, scrub the skin in warm soapy water and rinse well before use.) Chillies, spring onions, and root ginger keep best in airtight plastic bags in the fridge. It's also a good idea to wash and dry them before storage.

UNSALTED BUTTER	CHUNKS OF CHEDDAR AND GRUYERE	BUNCH OF SPRING ONIONS
MILK		
EGGS	TUB OF GOAT'S CHEESE	KNOB OF ROOT GINGER
TUBS OF CREME FRAICHE AND FROMAGE FRAIS	JAR OF MAYONNAISE	CUCUMBERS
	BACON	TOMATOES
CARTONS OF PLAIN YOGHURT AND GREEK YOGHURT	LEMONS AND LIMES	
CHUNK OF PARMESAN CHEESE	SMALL BAG OF FRESH RED AND GREEN CHILIES	

IN THE FREEZER

Pack away this small list of basics in the freezer and you'll find yourself ready, willing and able for all manner of emergencies. In addition, you could have a couple of standby prepared dishes on hand – throughout the book, those recipes that freeze well are indicated. Another good tip is to freeze a proportion of the nibbles you make each time you're entertaining. That way you can present a much wider selection with no extra effort!

PACKET OF SHORTCRUST PASTRY	PACKET OF SWEETCORN KERNELS	PACKET OF WHITE CRAB MEAT
PACKET OF PUFF PASTRY	PACKET OF PEAS	PACKET OF WHITE PITTA BREAD
BOX OF FILO PASTRY	PACKET OF SLICED SMOKED SALMON OR TROUT	PACKET OF MUFFINS
PACKET OF WHITE BREADCRUMBS	PACKET OF KIPPERS	LOAF OF BROWN AND/OR WHITE BREAD
PACKET OF LEAF SPINACH	PACKET OF LARGE PRAWNS	

ON THE WINDOWSILL

Whenever possible, you should use fresh herbs for their powerful and pungent flavours. Buying them in small plastic packets from the supermarket or greengrocer can be very expensive, so try growing a good selection of herbs on the windowsill. They look so attractive too.

Parsley and chives are essential, while basil, thyme, mint, tarragon, rosemary, dill, and oregano are all useful additions. Herbs just need to be watered occasionally to thrive, and picking the new shoots encourages the plant to fill out.

IN THE VEGETABLE RACK

Vegetables with a very long shelf life include potatoes, shallots, onions, carrots, and garlic. No doubt you already have a high turnover of most of these. For storage, remove them from their original packaging and discard any damaged produce to prevent further decay. All these vegetables will keep well in a cool, dark place, such as a garage or shed, preferably stored on individual wire racks. Onions, shallots, and garlic can also be hung up in bunches in any dry, airy place. Braids of these vegetables make an attractive kitchen ornament, but exposure to the light and humidity of a kitchen will diminish their keeping power and flavour. Covered terracotta containers with ventilation holes offer an alternative storage method that is both attractive and practical where cupboard space is limited.

Always buy the freshest vegetables you can find and make the most of seasonal produce. Not only does it taste great at its peak, but it will also be very reasonable in price. Nowadays it's hard to be aware of the seasons changing, as most things seem to be available all year round, so don't be afraid to get to know your grocer and ask his or her advice – you'll be an expert in no time at all!

IN THE DRINKS CABINET

A well-stocked drinks cabinet may seem an extravagance, but it is a real asset to any cook. Having a selection available will encourage you to experiment with different flavourings – just a dash of something can make all the difference to a dish.

It is always a good idea to have a bottle of red or dry white cooking wine on hand, but skimping on the quality will lessen the flavour of the final dish. Half bottles are ideal for this purpose and they can be sealed for storage with an airtight vacuum seal, specially designed to prolong the shelf life of opened wines.

Unlike wine, it's perfectly acceptable to use cheaper, unknown brands of spirits in cooking. Some supermarkets cater for this with their 'own label' brands of the basics like brandy, rum, vermouth, and sherry, sold at reasonable prices. Miniatures are also very handy to have on hand, particularly of the spirits and liqueurs you don't use too often. But remember that alcohol, like many other ingredients, has a use-by date, and beyond that time it won't add much flavour to your cooking.

THE RECIPES

HOT & SPICY

These recipes are drawn from all around the globe and are for anyone who likes a bit of a kick to their food. As 'hotness' is very much a matter of personal taste, always use chillies with caution, because they vary enormously in strength. However, appearance can give you some clues. Dark green chillies are usually hotter than pale green or red ones. Also, the sharply pointed thin chillies tend to be hotter than short blunt ones, which are the kind that were used in testing the recipes. All recipes serve 4–6.

THAI CRAB BITES WITH SPICED COCONUT DIP

To make this in advance, arrange the cooked crab bites on a baking tray and the dip in a bowl, then leave to cool completely. Cover with cling film and chill for up to 24 hours (the crab bites can also be frozen). Reheat the crab bites at 200°C/400°F/Gas 6 for about 10 minutes.

450g/1lb white crab meat, thawed and well drained if frozen
1 stalk lemon grass, finely chopped
2 red chillies, seeded and chopped
2 tbsp chopped fresh coriander
1 egg yolk
2 tbsp double cream
1 tsp cornflour
vegetable oil, for deep-frying

FOR THE SPICED COCONUT DIP
1 tbsp sesame oil
4 spring onions, finely chopped
1 tbsp Thai red curry paste
400g/14oz can coconut milk
1 tbsp light soy sauce

Place the crab meat in a bowl with the lemon grass, chillies, coriander and egg yolk. Heat the cream with the cornflour until thickened, and mix with the crab mixture until well combined. Shape into about 20 walnut-sized balls, squeezing out any excess moisture. Place on a plate and chill for at least 15 minutes, and up to 12 hours, to allow the balls to firm up.

Meanwhile, make the spiced coconut dip: heat the oil in a saucepan and fry the spring onions for 30 seconds. Stir in the curry paste and cook for 1 minute. Pour in the coconut milk and bring to the boil. Simmer for 15–20 minutes or until reduced by half and thickened. Stir in the soy sauce, pour into a serving bowl and leave to cool.

Heat oil to 180°C/350°F or until a cube of bread will brown in 30 seconds. Deep-fry the crab bites in batches for 3–4 minutes or until crisp and golden brown. Remove with a slotted spoon and drain on kitchen paper. Serve warm, with the dip.

POLENTA BISCUITS WITH ROASTED TOMATO SALSA

These biscuits are based on an old American recipe. They are the perfect foil for the richness of the roasted tomato salsa. Roasting tomatoes intensifies and almost caramelises their flavour – you'll be hooked once you've tried them!

175g/6oz easy-cook polenta
1/2 tsp chilli powder
50g/2oz butter, melted, plus extra for greasing

FOR THE ROASTED TOMATO SALSA
450g/1lb ripe plum tomatoes
2 shallots, peeled
2 garlic cloves, peeled
1 red chilli, halved and seeded
salt and freshly ground black pepper
3 tbsp extra-virgin olive oil
1/2 tsp chopped fresh rosemary
juice of 1 lemon
1 tsp caster sugar

Preheat the oven to 200°C/400°F/Gas 6. To make the salsa, place the tomatoes, shallots, garlic and chilli in a roasting tin. Season well and roast for 40–45 minutes or until the tomatoes have started to blacken.

Meanwhile, put 750ml/1¼ pints of water in a saucepan with a good pinch of salt and bring to the boil. Pour in the polenta in a continuous stream, stirring constantly to prevent any lumps forming. Add the chilli powder. Cook for 5 minutes, stirring constantly, and then remove from the heat.

Stir in the butter. Spoon heaped tablespoons of the polenta mixture on to large buttered baking trays – you should make about 20 biscuits in all. Bake for 25–30 minutes or until the edges are crisp and beginning to brown. Transfer to wire racks and leave to cool and crisp up.

When the tomatoes are ready, scoop out all the seeds and juice. Chop the pulp with the shallots, garlic and chilli, discarding any burnt bits. Place in a small serving bowl and add the oil, rosemary, lemon juice, sugar and any juices from the pan. Season generously. Serve at room temperature with the polenta biscuits.

Above: Sweet Potato Discs with Chilli Butter Dip

VEGETABLE TEMPURA WITH CHILLI DIPPING SAUCE

The beer in this batter makes a wonderful light, crisp coating for the vegetables. However, you could substitute chilled water.

2 eggs	FOR THE CHILLI DIPPING SAUCE
300ml/10floz chilled light ale	6 tbsp light soy sauce
225g/8oz plain flour, plus extra for dusting	1 red chilli, seeded and finely chopped
4 small courgettes	1 tsp sugar
2 large red peppers, halved and seeded	2.5cm/1in piece root ginger, finely shredded
450g/1lb broccoli	
vegetable oil, for deep-frying	

To make the sauce: mix together the soy sauce, chilli, sugar and ginger and pour into a small serving bowl. To make the batter, lightly whisk together the eggs and light ale. Tip in the flour all at once and whisk quickly until the batter is smooth.

Cut the courgettes across in half, then cut each half into four sticks. Cut each pepper half into 12 pieces. Break the broccoli into florets.

Heat oil to 180°C/350°F or until a cube of bread will brown in 30 seconds. While the oil is heating, place a little flour on a plate.

Coat the vegetables lightly with flour, then dip into the batter. Deep-fry in batches for 3–4 minutes or until crisp and golden. Drain on kitchen paper. Serve at once, with the dipping sauce.

MEXICAN LAMB FAJITAS

You could use any combination of vegetables for this recipe, such as baby sweetcorn, spring onions, or carrot or celery matchsticks.

450g/1lb lean lamb fillet	1 red and 1 yellow pepper, seeded and sliced
2 garlic cloves, crushed	1 courgette, cut into matchsticks
2 tsp chilli powder	salt and freshly ground black pepper
2 tsp sun-dried tomato paste	8 soft flour tortillas
2 tbsp sunflower oil	120ml/4fl oz soured cream
1 large onion, thickly sliced	

Cut the lamb into thin slices, discarding any fat, and place in a bowl. Add the garlic, chilli powder and sun-dried tomato paste and mix well.

Heat the oil in a large pan and fry the lamb for 4–5 minutes or until lightly browned. Add the onion, peppers and courgette and stir-fry for another 3–4 minutes or until the onion is just cooked through. Season to taste.

Wrap the flour tortillas in a tea towel and place in a steamer for a couple of minutes until heated through. Spoon some of the lamb mixture down the middle of each tortilla. Drizzle a tablespoon of the soured cream down each one, then roll up and cut in half to serve.

SWEET POTATO DISCS WITH CHILLI BUTTER DIP

There are two main types of sweet potatoes. Both are suitable for this recipe, although the orange-fleshed variety has a more dramatic colour and sweeter flavour than the pale yellow type.

4 sweet potatoes, each about 225g/8oz
vegetable oil, for deep-frying

FOR THE CHILLI BUTTER DIP

75g/3oz unsalted butter	1 tsp sun-dried tomato paste
1 garlic clove, crushed	2 tbsp chopped mixed fresh herbs, such as
1 small shallot, finely chopped	thyme, parsley and chives
2 small red chillies, seeded and	salt and freshly ground black pepper
finely chopped	

Peel the sweet potatoes and cut into discs about 5mm/1/4in thick. Rinse under cold running water and pat dry on kitchen paper. Heat oil to 180°C/350°F or until a cube of bread will brown in 30 seconds.

While the oil is heating, make the chilli butter dip: melt the butter very gently in a small pan. Add the garlic, shallot, chillies and sun-dried tomato paste and cook over a very low heat for about 5 minutes or until the shallot has softened. Remove from the heat, stir in the herbs and season to taste. Pour into a small bowl and leave at room temperature (don't leave it too long or the butter will harden).

Add the sweet potato discs to the hot oil and deep fry for 4–5 minutes or until tender and golden. Remove with a slotted spoon and drain on kitchen paper. Arrange on a serving platter and season to taste. Serve hot, with the chilli butter dip.

GUACAMOLE WITH ROASTED PEPPERS AND CHILLI TORTILLA CHIPS

If you want to make the guacamole in advance, drizzle a little more lime juice over the surface and cover tightly with cling film.

1 small red and 1 small yellow pepper
1 large ripe avocado
100g/4oz tomatoes, seeded and diced
2 spring onions, finely chopped

juice of 1 lime
1/2 tsp each garlic salt and chilli powder
225g/8oz packet chilli tortilla chips

Preheat the grill. Cut the peppers in half and then into quarters. Remove the seeds. Grill, skin side up, until the skins have blackened and blistered. Remove from the heat and leave to cool a little, then pull away the skins and cut the flesh into small dice.

Cut the avocado in half and remove the stone. Scoop the flesh into a non-metallic dish and mash to a fairly smooth purée. Stir in the diced peppers, tomatoes and spring onions. Add the lime juice, garlic salt and chilli powder and mix well. Cover and chill until ready to serve, with the tortilla chips.

VEGETABLE BHAJIAS WITH TOMATO CHUTNEY

These can be made and cooked several hours in advance. Just before serving, reheat the bhajias in a preheated 200°C/400°F/Gas 6 oven for 8–10 minutes. Or you could deep-fry them for another 1–2 minutes.

150g/5oz gram flour (chickpea flour), plus extra for dusting
1/2 tsp bicarbonate of soda
2 tsp medium-hot curry powder
vegetable oil, for deep-frying
1 aubergine, cut into discs
1 sweet potato, cut into discs
450g/1lb cauliflower, broken into small florets

FOR THE TOMATO CHUTNEY
2 tbsp vegetable oil
2 tsp cumin seeds
1 large onion, chopped
400g/14oz can chopped tomatoes
2 tbsp sugar
1 tbsp red wine vinegar
salt and freshly ground black pepper

Sift the flour, bicarbonate of soda, curry powder and a pinch of salt into a large bowl. Gradually stir in 250ml/8fl oz of water to make a smooth batter. Cover and leave to rest for 15 minutes.

Meanwhile, make the chutney: heat the oil in a saucepan and fry the cumin seeds for 20 seconds or until they start to splutter. Add the onion and fry gently until softened. Stir in the tomatoes, sugar and vinegar and season generously. Simmer for 15 minutes or until reduced and thickened. Leave to cool.

Heat oil to 180C/350F or until a cube of bread will brown in 30 seconds. While the oil is heating, cut the aubergine and sweet potato discs in half to make half-moons. Place a little gram flour on a plate.

Dust all the vegetables in gram flour, then dip in the batter. Deep-fry in batches for 5 minutes or until golden. Remove with a slotted spoon and drain on kitchen paper. Serve hot, with the chutney.

CHINESE PANCAKE ROLLS

Spring roll wrappers are sold fresh or frozen in Oriental supermarkets and delicatessens.

1 tbsp sunflower oil
1 garlic clove, finely chopped
1cm/1/2in piece root ginger, finely chopped
6 spring onions, finely chopped
225g/8oz cooked peeled prawns
1 tbsp soy sauce, plus extra for dipping

1/2 tsp sugar
12 spring roll wrappers, thawed if frozen
150g/5oz beansprouts
1/2 small red chilli, finely chopped
vegetable oil, for deep-frying

Heat the oil in a small pan and fry the garlic and ginger for 1 minute. Add the spring onions, prawns, soy sauce and sugar and cook for 1–2 minutes, stirring continuously. Add the beansprouts and chilli and stir-fry for 30 seconds. Remove from the heat, tip into a sieve and place over the pan to drain – the mixture must be very dry.

Place one of the spring roll wrappers on the work surface at an angle so one corner points at you. Spoon a heaped tablespoon of the filling near the bottom corner of the wrapper. Fold up the bottom and fold in the sides, then roll from the bottom upwards, moistening with a little water and pressing to seal. Repeat to fill and shape the remaining rolls.

Heat vegetable oil to 180°C/350°F or until a cube of bread will brown in 30 seconds. Deep-fry the pancake rolls for 2–3 minutes or until crisp and golden brown all over. Remove with a slotted spoon and drain on kitchen paper. Serve hot, with soy sauce for dipping.

Above: Vegetable Tempura with Chilli Dipping Sauce

POTATO WEDGES WITH FRESH CORIANDER CHUTNEY

You can make this chutney very quickly in a food processor – just put in all the ingredients (there is no need to chop anything first) and blend to a thick paste.

2 tbsp sunflower oil	FOR THE CHUTNEY
4 baking potatoes, each about 225g/8oz	25g/1oz chopped fresh coriander
2 tsp hot curry powder	1 shallot, finely chopped
1 tsp coarse sea salt	juice of 1 lemon
	1/2 tsp chilli powder
	1 tsp ground cumin

Preheat the oven to 200°C/400°F/Gas 6. Heat the oil in a large baking tray in the oven for 5 minutes. Cut each potato into eight wedges, rinse under cold running water and pat dry with kitchen paper.

Add the potato wedges to the heated oil in the baking tray. Toss until well coated and then sprinkle over the curry powder. Bake for 30–35 minutes or until golden brown, turning halfway through cooking.

Meanwhile, make the chutney: mix together the coriander, shallot, lemon juice, chilli powder and cumin in a small serving bowl.

When the potatoes are cooked, sprinkle with the salt and serve hot, with the chutney.

SPICED LAMB SKEWERS WITH TZATZIKI

A food processor can save a lot of time in preparing this recipe. Simply blend the lamb, onion and parsley, then add the remaining ingredients and blend again to make a sticky paste.

450g/1lb lean minced lamb	FOR THE TZATZIKI
1 onion, finely chopped	150ml/5floz plain yoghurt
25g/1oz fresh parsley, chopped	10cm/4in piece cucumber, seeded and diced
1 tsp ground coriander	2 tbsp chopped fresh mint
1/2 tsp each ground mixed spice and	1 garlic clove, crushed
chilli powder	salt and freshly ground black pepper

To make the tzatziki, place the yoghurt, cucumber, mint and garlic in a small bowl and mix well. Season to taste. Cover with cling film and chill until ready to use.

Put the lamb, onion and parsley in a bowl and mix until well combined. Add the coriander, mixed spice and chilli powder, season generously and mix well again.

Preheat the grill. Divide the lamb mixture into eight portions and roll each into a sausage shape about 10cm/4in long. Thread each sausage on to a metal skewer about 15cm/6in long. Grill for 8–10 minutes, turning occasionally, until cooked through but still moist. Serve hot, with the tzatziki.

HOT AND SOUR NOODLE-WRAPPED PRAWNS

Large raw prawns are now readily available in fishmongers and at the wet fish counters in supermarkets. However, if you can't get hold of any, use large cooked peeled prawns and grill for just 2–3 minutes.

450g/1lb large raw tiger or king prawns	juice of 3 limes
2 red chillies, seeded and finely chopped	2 tbsp light soy sauce
2 garlic cloves, crushed	2 tsp sesame oil
1 stalk lemon grass, crushed	25g/1oz dried medium egg noodles
2 tbsp chopped fresh coriander	

Peel the prawns, leaving the tails intact. Mix together the chillies, garlic, lemon grass, coriander, lime juice, soy sauce and sesame oil in a shallow non-metallic dish. Add the prawns and turn to coat. Cover with cling film and chill for at least 15 minutes and up to 1 hour.

Cook the noodles in a pan of boiling salted water for 1 minute or until just softened. Drain and refresh under cold running water. Wrap a piece of noodle around each prawn and arrange on a lightly greased baking tray.

Place the marinade in a small pan and bring to the boil. Simmer for 1–2 minutes, then pour into a serving bowl and leave to cool.

Preheat the grill. Grill the prawns for 5–6 minutes, turning once, until just cooked through. Serve at once, with the dipping sauce.

CHINESE-SPICED SPARE RIBS

The ribs are first simmered to tenderise the meat before being roasted in a Chinese-spiced sauce. Remember to give each guest a finger bowl of warm water because eating ribs can be a messy business.

1kg/2lb meaty pork spare ribs	1 tsp Chinese five-spice powder
2 tbsp red wine vinegar	6 tbsp dark soy sauce
1 tbsp sesame oil	juice of 1 lemon
2 garlic cloves, crushed	4 tbsp clear honey
2.5cm/1in piece root ginger, crushed	

Place the ribs in a large saucepan and pour over enough water to cover. Add the vinegar, bring to the boil and simmer for 20 minutes, skimming occasionally to remove any scum. Drain and tip into a large roasting tin.

Preheat the oven to 200°C/400°F/Gas 6. Heat the oil in a small pan and fry the garlic and ginger for 10 seconds. Stir in the Chinese five-spice powder and cook for another 10 seconds, stirring. Add the soy sauce, lemon juice, honey and 120ml/4fl oz of water. Bring to the boil, then simmer for 5 minutes or until reduced and thickened slightly.

Pour the sauce over the ribs and turn to coat evenly. Roast for about 1 hour, basting every 10 minutes. Leave to cool for about 5 minutes before serving.

Right: Hot and Sour Noodle-Wrapped Prawns

SWEETCORN AND CHILLI CORNBREAD MUFFINS

You could use fresh sweetcorn for this recipe. Hold one end of the cob, place the other end on a chopping board, and slice down the side of the cob with a sharp knife to cut off the kernels. Makes 20

175g/6oz plain flour
1 tbsp baking powder
1 tsp salt
100g/4oz cornmeal
2 eggs, beaten

300ml/10floz buttermilk
2 tbsp sunflower oil, plus extra for brushing
175g/6oz sweetcorn, thawed if frozen
2 green chillies, seeded and finely chopped
50g/2oz Parmesan, freshly grated

Preheat the oven to 200°C/400°F/Gas 6. Sift the flour, baking powder and salt into a large bowl. Stir in the cornmeal. Mix together the eggs, buttermilk and oil and stir into the dry ingredients. Add the sweetcorn, chillies and Parmesan and mix until well combined.

Place paper cases in 20 bun tins and brush generously with oil. Spoon in the sweetcorn mixture, almost filling each paper case. Bake for 25–30 minutes or until risen and golden brown. Serve warm or cold.

FRIED CAULIFLOWER FLORETS WITH ROMESCO SAUCE

This traditional Spanish sauce has many variations. It works wonderfully with the crisp, marinated cauliflower.

450g/1lb cauliflower, cut into florets
4 tbsp white wine vinegar
4 tbsp chopped fresh parsley
salt and freshly ground black pepper
1 red pepper, seeded and quartered
225g/8oz small tomatoes

8 tbsp olive oil
2 garlic cloves, crushed
1 red chilli, seeded and finely chopped
1 slice stale white bread, broken into pieces
50g/2oz flaked almonds, toasted
2 eggs, beaten

Put the cauliflower florets in a large bowl. Sprinkle over 2 tablespoons of water and add half the vinegar and parsley. Season to taste and mix well. Cover with cling film and set aside for at least 15 minutes and up to 30 minutes, stirring occasionally.

Meanwhile, make the romesco sauce: preheat the grill and grill the pepper and tomatoes until the skins are charred. Leave to cool slightly, then remove the skins and discard. Cut the tomatoes in half, scoop out the seeds and chop the flesh with the pepper flesh.

Heat 2 tablespoons of the oil in a frying pan and gently fry the garlic and chilli for 1–2 minutes. Add the bread and fry until lightly browned. Place the bread mixture in a food processor with the tomato and pepper flesh, the remaining vinegar and parsley, and the almonds. Blend to a rough purée. Then, with the motor running, add 4 tablespoons of the oil in a thin, steady stream. Pour the sauce into a small serving bowl and season to taste.

Heat the remaining oil in a large frying pan. Drain the cauliflower and pat dry. Dip into the beaten eggs and stir-fry for about 10 minutes or until tender and lightly golden. Serve at once, with the romesco sauce.

EMPANADAS

These can be made up to 24 hours in advance, then covered with cling film and stored in the fridge. Don't worry if they go a little soggy – they will crisp up once reheated. Arrange on a baking tray and bake in a preheated 200°C/400°F/Gas 6 oven for 8–10 minutes.

1 tbsp sunflower oil
1 red and 1 green chilli, seeded and finely chopped
1 tsp cumin seeds
225g/8oz sweetcorn, thawed if frozen
2 plum tomatoes, peeled, seeded and diced
50g/2oz Cheddar cheese, grated
salt and freshly ground black pepper
vegetable oil, for frying

FOR THE PASTRY
225g/8oz plain flour
1 tsp salt
50g/2oz white vegetable fat, diced

To make the pastry, sift the flour and salt into a bowl and rub in the fat. Gradually add 150ml/5floz of warm water and mix to a soft dough. Turn out on to a lightly floured surface and knead for 2–3 minutes. Wrap in cling film and leave in the fridge for 15 minutes.

Meanwhile, heat the sunflower oil in a pan and fry the chillies and cumin for 2 minutes. Remove from the heat and add the sweetcorn, tomatoes and cheese. Mix well and leave to cool. Season to taste.

Roll out the pastry dough on a lightly floured surface and stamp out 20 rounds using a 10cm/4in cutter. Place a tablespoon of the sweetcorn mixture on each round. Dampen the pastry edges with water, then fold in half and press the edges to seal.

Heat about 1cm/$\frac{1}{2}$in of oil in a frying pan and fry the empanadas in batches for about 5 minutes or until golden brown, turning once. Remove with a slotted spoon and drain on kitchen paper. Serve hot.

BARBECUE-HOT CHICKEN WINGS

Chicken wings are very cheap to buy and are also a great finger food – just make sure you have plenty of napkins for sticky fingers!

3 tbsp tomato ketchup
1 tbsp chilli sauce
1 tsp Worcestershire sauce
2 garlic cloves, crushed

1 tsp light muscovado sugar
1 tsp prepared English mustard
12 chicken wings

Put the tomato ketchup, chilli sauce, Worcestershire sauce, garlic, sugar and mustard in a shallow non-metallic dish and mix well.

Remove the thin pointy tip from each chicken wing, leaving just the elbow and mini drumstick. Add the chicken wings to the marinade and turn to coat. Cover with cling film and chill for at least 15 minutes and up to 24 hours.

Preheat the grill. Shake any excess marinade from the chicken wings and place them on a rack in a grill pan. Grill for 15–20 minutes, turning occasionally, until crisp and cooked through. Serve hot.

Right: Barbecue-Hot Chicken Wings

MINI SAMOSAS WITH MINT AND CORIANDER CHUTNEY

Filo pastry is extremely thin and almost transparent, and it can be slightly tricky to handle. It's a good idea to keep the pastry sheets covered with a damp tea towel, to prevent any cracking or drying out.

6 tbsp sunflower oil
1 garlic clove, crushed
1cm/1/2in piece root ginger, crushed
350g/12oz potatoes, diced
1 tbsp medium curry paste
75g/3oz peas, thawed if frozen
4 sheets filo pastry, thawed if frozen

FOR THE CHUTNEY
15g/1/2oz each chopped fresh mint and coriander
1 red chilli, seeded and finely chopped
juice of 1 lime
1 tsp garam masala

Preheat the oven to 200°C/400°F/Gas 6. Heat half the oil in a frying pan and fry the garlic and ginger for 10 seconds. Add the potatoes, stir well, cover and cook for 10 minutes or until tender, stirring frequently.

Stir in the curry paste and peas and cook for a further 2–3 minutes. Remove from the heat and leave to cool completely.

Meanwhile, make the chutney: mix together the mint, coriander, chilli, lime juice and garam masala in a small bowl. Set aside.

Cut each sheet of filo into three equal pieces. Take one piece and place a tablespoon of the vegetable mixture at one end. Brush the pastry edges lightly with oil. Fold a bottom corner diagonally over the filling, then fold this triangle over on itself two times to make a neat parcel. Repeat to make 12 triangles in all.

Place the samosas on a lightly greased baking tray and brush with the remaining oil. Bake for about 20 minutes or until crisp and golden brown. Serve hot, with the chutney.

TURKEY WONTONS

These are a Chinese version of ravioli. They can be deep-fried for 2–3 minutes, but are softer when steamed. Wonton papers, which are about 7.5cm/3in square, are sold fresh or frozen in Oriental shops.

1 tbsp sunflower oil
4 spring onions, finely chopped
75g/3oz cooked turkey breast, finely chopped
100g/4oz beansprouts, chopped
2 garlic cloves, crushed
2.5cm/1in piece root ginger, crushed
1 tbsp light soy sauce, plus extra for dipping
1 tsp clear honey
1 tsp sesame oil
20 wonton papers, thawed if frozen

Heat the sunflower oil in a pan and fry the spring onions for 10 seconds. Remove from the heat and add the turkey, beansprouts, garlic, ginger, soy sauce, honey and sesame oil. Mix well.

Place a heaped teaspoon of the turkey mixture into the middle of a wonton paper. Dampen the edges with water and bring two opposite edges up to overlap in the centre. Bring up the remaining edges to form a purse shape, pinching together to seal. Repeat until you have 20 wontons.

Place the turkey wontons in a single layer in a lightly oiled steamer and steam for 6–8 minutes or until tender and heated through. Serve at once, with soy sauce for dipping.

PLANTAIN CHIPS WITH TAMARIND CHUTNEY

Indian and Thai shops sell tamarind paste in jars as well as semi-dried tamarind in blocks. The latter needs to be broken up, soaked in boiling water and pushed through a sieve to make a thick paste.

2 unripe green plantains, peeled and cut into thin slices
vegetable oil, for deep-frying

FOR THE TAMARIND CHUTNEY
2 tbsp sunflower oil
1 onion, finely chopped
2 green chillies, seeded and finely chopped
5cm/2in piece root ginger, finely chopped
1 tsp hot curry paste
5 tbsp tamarind paste
1 tsp salt
1 tbsp light muscovado sugar

Rinse the plantains in cold water and pat dry. Heat oil to 180°C/350°F or until a bread cube will brown in 30 seconds. Deep-fry the plantain chips in batches for 4–5 minutes or until cooked and lightly golden. Drain on kitchen paper and leave to cool.

To make the chutney, heat the oil in a pan and fry the onion, chillies and ginger for 4–5 minutes or until the onion has softened. Stir in the curry paste and cook for another minute, then stir in the tamarind paste, salt, sugar and 150ml/5floz of water. Simmer for 10–15 minutes or until thickened. Leave to cool, then serve with the plantain chips.

MIXED SATAY SKEWERS

Indonesian spice powder, otherwise known as Laos powder, is now sold in supermarkets under well-known brand labels.

1 chicken breast fillet, skinned
175g/6oz each pork fillet and rump steak
1 garlic clove, crushed
1 tbsp light muscovado sugar
1 tbsp Indonesian spice powder
4 tbsp coconut milk
salt and freshly ground white pepper

FOR THE PEANUT SAUCE
300ml/10floz coconut milk
4 tbsp peanut butter
2 tbsp Thai green curry paste
2 tbsp light muscovado sugar
juice of 1 lime

Using a sharp knife, cut the chicken breast in half horizontally, then in half lengthways, to make four pieces. Cut the pork and steak into 2.5cm/1in slices on the diagonal. Place all the meat between two sheets of cling film and beat with a rolling pin to flatten. Cut each piece in half lengthways and place in a shallow non-metallic dish.

Mix together the garlic, sugar, Indonesian spice, coconut milk and seasoning to make a fairly thick paste. Spoon over the meat and turn to coat. Leave to marinate for at least 15 minutes and up to 24 hours.

To make the sauce, place all the ingredients in a pan and bring to the boil. Simmer for about 10 minutes or until thickened. Season to taste, then leave to cool.

Preheat the grill. Thread the meat on to 15cm/6in bamboo skewers and brush with a little oil. Grill for about 10 minutes, turning frequently, until cooked through. Serve hot, with the peanut sauce.

Right: Mini Samosas with Mint and Coriander Chutney

FANCY FINGER FOOD

Small nibbles can take hours of preparation, only to be devoured by your guests in moments. The great thing about the recipes in this chapter is that you can prepare most of them, ready to cook, up to 24 hours in advance, or you can have them tucked away in the freezer, ready for any eventuality. As a general rule when entertaining, allow about 12 nibbles per person, and prepare a few different recipes to give variety. Arrange them on large serving platters, mixing and matching the colours, shapes and flavours. Give your guests napkins, and leave plenty of small plates or ashtrays around so that people can discard any unwanted bits and pieces. All recipes make 24 portions.

SALT COD FRITTERS WITH SWEET PEPPER SAUCE

This can be prepared several hours in advance. Cover the dip and chill until needed. Cook the fritters according to the recipe, drain well on kitchen paper, cover and chill. Just before serving, reheat in a hot oven for about 5 minutes.

675g/1¹/2lb salt cod	FOR THE SWEET PEPPER SAUCE
600ml/1 pint milk	2 tbsp olive oil
100g/4oz plain flour, plus extra for dusting	4 large garlic cloves
120ml/4floz light ale	400g/14oz can sweet peppers (pimientos),
1 egg, beaten	rinsed and drained
2 tbsp chopped fresh parsley	4 tbsp fromage frais
vegetable oil, for deep-frying	salt and freshly ground black pepper

Rinse the salt cod under cold running water, then place in a bowl and cover with cold water. Leave to soak for 12 hours, changing the water every couple of hours. Drain, rinse again under cold running water and pat dry with kitchen paper. Remove the skin and cut the flesh into 24 cubes. Place in a bowl, pour over 450ml/15floz of the milk and leave for 2 hours. Drain, rinse again and pat dry.

To make the sweet pepper sauce, heat the olive oil in a pan and fry the unpeeled garlic cloves for 2–3 minutes or until golden. Add 2 tablespoons of water, cover and simmer gently for 15 minutes or until completely softened. Squeeze the garlic flesh into a food processor and add the peppers and fromage frais. Blend until smooth and season to taste. Transfer to a small serving bowl and chill until needed.

Sift the flour and 1 teaspoon salt into a large bowl and make a well in the centre. Gradually beat in the remaining milk, light ale and egg to form a smooth batter. Stir in the parsley. Leave to rest for 30 minutes.

Heat oil to 180°C/350°F or until a cube of bread will brown in 30 seconds. Dust the salt cod cubes in a little flour, dip into the batter and deep-fry in batches for about 5 minutes or until crisp and golden brown. Drain on kitchen paper and serve warm, with the sauce.

MINI BOEUF EN CROÛTE

These can be made several hours in advance and just popped in the oven when you are ready for them. Don't let them hang around for too long after you have taken them out of the oven, because the steak will continue to cook and the pastry can become a bit soggy.

1 large onion	2 tbsp brandy
225g/8oz open-cap mushrooms	salt and freshly ground black pepper
25g/1oz butter	500g/1lb 2oz puff pastry, thawed if frozen
675g/1¹/2lb fillet steak, in one piece	1 egg, beaten
1 tbsp sunflower oil, plus extra for greasing	

Place the onion and mushrooms in a food processor and blend until very finely chopped. Melt the butter in a pan and gently fry the onion and mushroom mixture for 10–15 minutes or until all the liquid has evaporated. Leave to cool.

Trim the fillet steak and cut into 24 cubes, 4cm/1¹/2in wide and 1cm/¹/2in thick. Heat the oil in a heavy-based frying pan until very hot and fry the beef for about 5 seconds on each side or until sealed but not at all cooked. It is best to do this in batches. Leave to cool completely, then brush with the brandy and season well.

Roll out the pastry on a lightly floured board to a 3mm/¹/8in thickness and cut into 10cm/4in squares. Brush each square lightly with beaten egg and place ¹/2 teaspoon of the onion mixture in the middle. Add a cube of beef and top each with ¹/2 teaspoon of the onion mixture.

Pat each mound of filling into a neat shape, then bring two opposite corners of pastry up to overlap in the centre, tucking in the sides. Brush the pastry all over with more beaten egg and bring the two remaining corners up to overlap each other. Seal gently and and chill for at least 30 minutes and up to 24 hours.

Preheat the oven to 220°C/425°F/Gas 7 and heat two baking trays. When the trays are hot, brush them with oil and sprinkle lightly with water. Arrange the parcels on the baking trays and bake for 10–15 minutes or until golden brown. Serve hot.

Above: Pancetta and Gruyère Tartlets

PANCETTA AND GRUYÈRE TARTLETS

These tartlets can be frozen for up to 1 month. Cool quickly, pack into a rigid plastic container and cover before freezing. Pancetta is Italian streaky bacon, available from delicatessens. If you can't get any, you can use normal streaky bacon instead.

200g/7oz filo pastry, thawed if frozen	*175g/6oz pancetta, finely chopped*
50g/2oz butter, melted	*4 eggs, beaten*
175g/6oz Gruyère cheese, finely grated	*175ml/6fl oz milk*
1 tbsp olive oil	*6 tbsp double cream*
2 garlic cloves, crushed	*salt and freshly ground black pepper*

Preheat the oven to 180°C/350°F/Gas 4. Cut the sheets of filo into 7.5cm/3in squares and keep covered with a damp tea towel. Place a filo square in each of 24 bun tins and brush with a little of the butter. Layer another two squares in each bun tin, arranging them at angles to give a star effect and brushing with the butter as you go. Sprinkle over half of the Gruyère.

Heat the oil in a small frying pan and fry the garlic for 1 minute. Add the pancetta and cook until lightly browned. Leave to cool. Beat together the eggs, milk, cream and seasoning and stir in the pancetta.

Spoon the pancetta mixture into the filo cases and sprinkle over the remaining Gruyère. Bake for 15–20 minutes or until the pastry is crisp and the filling has set. Leave to cool a little on a wire rack and serve warm or at room temperature.

CAVIAR CANAPÉS

The bases of these canapés are blinis, the yeasty pancakes made from buckwheat flour. Originally from Russia, they make the perfect accompaniment for soured cream and caviar.

450ml/15floz milk	*2 eggs, separated*
100g/4oz buckwheat flour	*sunflower oil, for brushing*
1 tbsp easy-blend dried yeast	*25g/1oz butter, melted*
1 tsp sugar	*150ml/5floz thick soured cream*
100g/4oz plain flour	*100g/4oz lumpfish roe or caviar*
pinch of salt	*1 tbsp snipped fresh chives*

Heat the milk in a small pan until just warm and remove from the heat. Place the buckwheat flour in a bowl and stir in the yeast and sugar. Gradually beat in half the warm milk.

Sift the plain flour and salt into a separate bowl, make a well in the centre and add the egg yolks and remaining warm milk. Beat well to make a smooth batter, then stir into the yeast mixture. Cover the bowl with cling film and leave to rise in a warm place until doubled in size, about 1 hour.

Whisk the egg whites in a clean bowl until stiff, then fold into the batter. Heat a heavy-based frying pan or griddle until hot and brush with some oil. Drop small spoonfuls of the batter on to the pan or griddle, spacing them a little apart, and cook until set and bubbles begin to appear on the surface. Turn the blinis over and cook for a further 30 seconds or until golden brown. Immediately brush one side of each blini with melted butter and leave to cool on a wire rack while you make the next batch.

Once all the blinis have cooled, top each one with a little soured cream and a teaspoon of caviar. Garnish with the chives and serve.

MARINATED HALLOUMI CHEESE AND TOMATO SKEWERS

These are great as there is very little effort involved. You could also thread them on to the cocktail sticks before marinating if you want to save some time later.

450g/1lb halloumi cheese	*1 tsp crushed mixed peppercorns*
350g/12oz small cherry tomatoes (about 24)	*1 tsp chopped fresh oregano*
2 tbsp extra-virgin olive oil	*2 tsp chopped fresh parsley*
1 small garlic clove, crushed	*juice of 1/2 lemon*

Cut the halloumi cheese into 1cm/1/2in cubes (there should be 48) and place in a shallow non-metallic dish with the cherry tomatoes. Add the oil, garlic, crushed peppercorns, oregano, parsley and lemon juice and mix well. Cover and leave to marinate in the fridge for at least 30 minutes and up to 24 hours.

Thread a cube of cheese on to a cocktail stick, then add a cherry tomato and another cube of cheese. Repeat until you have 24 skewers. Brush them with any remaining marinade. Serve at room temperature.

PESTO PASTRY TWISTS

You could also make these pastry twists with tapenade or some chopped mixed fresh herbs rather than pesto. To freeze, pack into a rigid plastic container and freeze for up to 3 months. To serve, defrost thoroughly on baking trays, then crisp up in a hot oven.

100g/4oz puff pastry, thawed if frozen
1 egg, beaten
1 tbsp pesto sauce

25g/1oz Parmesan, freshly grated
freshly ground black pepper

Roll out the pastry on a lightly floured surface to a rectangle about 3mm/1/8in thick. Brush with beaten egg and spread the pesto on top. Sprinkle over the Parmesan and season with pepper.

Fold the pastry rectangle in half to conceal the filling and press the edges down to seal well. Roll out to a 20cm/8in square and brush with beaten egg. Cut into 24 strips, about 5mm/1/4 in wide, discarding the ends. Twist each strip of pastry along its length and arrange on a lightly oiled baking tray, pressing the ends down flat. Chill for 15 minutes.

Preheat the oven to 200°C/400°F/Gas 6. Bake the twists for about 15 minutes or until golden and puffed up. Serve warm or cold.

MINI SPANAKOPITTA PURSES

To freeze the purses, pack them into a rigid plastic container; they can be kept in the freezer up to 1 month. Before serving, spread the purses on a baking tray and defrost for 1 hour before reheating in a 180°C/350°F/Gas 4 oven for 5–10 minutes.

1kg/2lb fresh spinach or 350g/12oz
frozen leaf spinach
100g/4oz butter
1 tbsp olive oil, plus extra for greasing
1 onion, finely chopped

good pinch of freshly grated nutmeg
24 sheets filo pastry, thawed if frozen
350g/12oz feta cheese, cut into
1cm/1/2in cubes
salt and freshly ground black pepper

Preheat the oven to 220°C/425°F/Gas 7. If the spinach is fresh, place it in a pan with a little boiling water and cook for 1–2 minutes, then drain well. If frozen, defrost gently and drain well. Mix the spinach with 25g/1oz of the butter. Heat the oil in a frying pan and fry the onion until softened, then add to the spinach with the nutmeg and mix well.

Cut the filo into 20 x 10cm/8 x 4in rectangles, then cut in half again to make 10cm/4in squares (there should be 48). Cover the filo with a damp tea towel.

Melt the remaining butter and brush a little over one square of filo. Put another square of filo on top, at right angles to the first, so you now have an eight-pointed star shape. Spoon a little of the spinach mixture in the middle of the filo star and put a couple of pieces of feta on top. Season to taste. Bring the points of the star together so they meet in the middle, and give a little twist to make a purse. Brush lightly with a little more melted butter. Repeat until you have 24 purses.

Arrange the purses on a lightly oiled baking tray and bake for about 15 minutes or until golden brown. Serve warm or at room temperature.

SUN-DRIED TOMATO AND CHICKEN BITES WITH BASIL MAYONNAISE

These are very easy to make using a food processor, but you could also make them by finely chopping the sun-dried tomatoes and olives.

200g/7oz jar sun-dried tomatoes
preserved in oil
50g/2oz pitted black olives
salt and freshly ground black pepper
500g/1lb 2oz skinless chicken fillets

50g/2oz fresh white breadcrumbs
2 tbsp chopped fresh parsley
120ml/4floz good-quality mayonnaise
2 tbsp shredded fresh basil leaves
2 tsp pesto sauce

Place the contents of the jar of sun-dried tomatoes and the olives in a food processor and blend to a rough purée. Season to taste. Cut the chicken into 2.5cm/1in cubes (there should be about 48) and place in a shallow non-metallic dish. Spread over the tomato and olive mixture, cover and leave to marinate in the fridge for at least 30 minutes and up to 24 hours.

Preheat the oven to 200°C/400°F/Gas 6. Mix together the breadcrumbs, parsley and seasoning in a small bowl. Thread two pieces of chicken on to each of 24 wooden cocktail sticks and sprinkle with the breadcrumb mixture. Arrange on a lightly oiled baking tray and bake for about 10 minutes or until the chicken is cooked.

Meanwhile, mix together the mayonnaise, basil, pesto and seasoning in a small serving bowl. Serve the chicken hot or cold, with the basil mayonnaise for dipping.

Above: *Sun-Dried Tomato and Chicken Bites with Basil Mayonnaise*

MINI POTATO CAKES WITH BACON AND BLUE CHEESE

These canapés literally take minutes to make. Potato cakes freeze very well and are a useful standby to keep in the freezer.

4 maple-cure back bacon rashers
175g/6oz blue cheese, such as Danish blue
12 potato cakes, thawed if frozen
25g/1oz butter, melted
1 tbsp chopped fresh parsley
freshly ground black pepper

Preheat the grill. Grill the bacon until crisp and golden, then snip into thin strips while still warm and set aside. Remove any rind from the cheese and cut into 2.5cm/1in slices (there should be 24 slices). Stamp out two 5cm/2in rounds from each potato cake, using a fluted metal cutter, and place on a rack in a foil-lined grill pan.

Toast the potato cakes on one side, then turn them over and brush lightly with the butter. Top each potato cake with a slice of cheese and grill until just melted and bubbling. Arrange the snipped bacon on top and sprinkle over the parsley. Season with pepper and serve at once.

MINIATURE SAVOURY CHOUX PUFFS

It is very important to split the cooked choux puffs as soon as they come out of the oven, to allow the steam to escape, then return them to the oven so that they can dry out completely.

75g/3oz plain flour
salt and freshly ground black pepper
40g/1 1/2oz butter
2 eggs, beaten
100g/4oz smoked streaky bacon rashers
100g/4oz garlic and herb cream cheese
150ml/5floz double cream

Preheat the oven to 190°C/375°F/Gas 5. Sift the flour and a good pinch of salt into a bowl. Place the butter in a pan with 150ml/5floz of water and heat gently until the butter has melted. Bring to the boil, then remove from the heat and tip in the flour and salt.

Beat well with a wooden spoon and continue beating over a low heat until the mixture thickens and leaves the sides of the pan in a ball. Remove from the heat and leave to cool slightly, then gradually beat in the eggs.

Drop 24 teaspoonfuls of the mixture on to dampened baking trays, spacing them slightly apart. Bake for about 15 minutes or until well risen and golden brown. Make a small slit in the side of each puff and return to the oven for 5 minutes. Leave to cool on a wire rack.

Preheat the grill and grill the bacon until crisp, then snip into small pieces. Beat the cream cheese with the cream until thickened and smooth. Stir in the bacon and season to taste.

Spoon the bacon filling into the choux buns and pile into a pyramid to serve.

SODA SCONES WITH SMOKED SALMON AND CHIVES

Scones freeze very well. Cool the cooked scones quickly, place in a rigid plastic container and freeze for up to 1 month. To serve, defrost at room temperature for 1 hour.

150g/5oz smoked salmon
(trimmings are fine)
120ml/4floz crème fraîche
2 tbsp snipped fresh chives
freshly ground black pepper

FOR THE SCONES
225g/8oz plain flour, plus extra
for dusting
1/2 tsp salt
1 tsp baking powder
40g/1 1/2oz butter
150ml/5floz buttermilk

Preheat the oven to 220°C/425°F/Gas 7. To make the scones, sift the flour, salt and baking powder into a bowl. Rub in the butter, then make a well in the centre and add the buttermilk. Mix to a soft dough and knead briefly on a lightly floured surface.

Roll out the dough to a 1cm/1/2in thickness and stamp out 12 rounds, using a 5cm/2in fluted cutter. Arrange slightly apart on a baking tray dusted with flour and bake for 12–15 minutes or until well risen and golden brown. Leave to cool on a wire rack.

Cut the smoked salmon into pieces. Split the scones in half and place a piece of salmon on each one. Spoon a little crème fraîche on top and sprinkle over some chives. Season with pepper and serve.

BLACK PUDDING TOASTS WITH APPLE

Don't be put off by thinking of black pudding as just a breakfast ingredient. The flavour combination of the mildly spiced apple, rich black pudding and nutty toast is a match made in heaven. Try to use a traditional variety of apple such as Russet or Cox's Orange Pippin.

2 firm eating apples, peeled,
cored and chopped
1/2 tsp mixed spice
1 tbsp double cream
1 tbsp Calvados
6 slices granary bread
50g/2oz butter, softened
225g/8oz black pudding
freshly ground black pepper
1 tbsp chopped fresh parsley

Place the apples, mixed spice and 2 tablespoons of water in a pan and bring to the boil. Simmer gently, stirring occasionally, until you have a rough purée. Stir in the cream and Calvados and heat through gently. Keep warm until needed.

Preheat the grill. Toast the slices of bread on both sides. Stamp out four rounds from each slice, using a 5cm/2in fluted cutter. Lightly butter the rounds and set aside. Cut the black pudding into 24 slices, and peel off and discard the outside skin. Grill for 1–2 minutes on each side or until just cooked through.

To serve, place a piece of black pudding on each round of toast and spoon some of the apple purée on top. Season with the pepper, sprinkle with the parsley and serve at once while still hot.

Right: Soda Scones with Smoked Salmon and Chives

PARMA HAM AND ROCKET CROSTINI

These are very simple to make and you can vary the toppings according to taste. Try cubed mozzarella or fontina cheese with sliced tomato and shredded basil, or sautéed mushrooms and walnuts topped with snipped fresh chives. They will all keep in the fridge for up to an hour before serving.

1 thin French baguette
5 tbsp extra-virgin olive oil
50g/2oz rocket leaves
1 tbsp red wine vinegar
salt and freshly ground black pepper
6 large slices Parma ham
25g/1oz Parmesan, cut into thin shavings

Preheat the grill. Cut the baguette into 24 slices, discarding the ends. Brush both sides of each slice with olive oil, using about 3 tablespoons in all, and grill for 8–10 minutes, turning once, until golden. Leave to cool on a wire rack.

Shred any large rocket leaves. Place the rocket in a bowl. To make the dressing, put the remaining oil in a screw-topped jar with the vinegar and seasoning. Shake to combine, then pour over the rocket and toss to coat all the leaves.

Top the toasts with a small handful of the dressed leaves. Cut each slice of Parma ham into four pieces and roll each one into a cigar shape. Place on the rocket leaves and garnish with the Parmesan shavings. Season with a little more pepper and serve.

ASPARAGUS BOREK

Borek is a Turkish term for a pastry-wrapped savoury. Try to buy ready-trimmed asparagus spears for this recipe, as they are exactly the right size and, therefore, there is no waste.

24 asparagus spears
12 sheets filo pastry, thawed if frozen
50g/2oz butter, melted
3 tbsp freshly grated Parmesan
salt and freshly ground black pepper

Preheat the oven to 200°C/400°F/Gas 6. Trim the asparagus spears to 10cm/4in lengths. Place in a pan of lightly salted boiling water and simmer for 2 minutes. Drain and refresh in cold running water. Pat dry with kitchen paper.

Cut the sheets of filo into 15cm/6in squares (there should be 24) and cover with a damp tea towel. Take one square of filo, brush with melted butter and sprinkle lightly with some of the Parmesan. Place an asparagus spear at one end of the square and season with pepper. Fold in the edges and roll up into a neat cigar shape, enclosing the asparagus completely. Brush with a little more of the melted butter and place on a lightly oiled baking tray. Repeat with the remaining ingredients to make 24 borek.

Bake for 10–12 minutes or until lightly golden. Serve hot.

MINIATURE SALMON CAKES WITH LEMON BUTTER SAUCE

You can make these 24 hours in advance; arrange on a baking tray, cover and chill until needed. They can be frozen for up to 1 month: quick-freeze on a baking tray, then pack into a rigid plastic container.

350g/12oz potatoes, cut into chunks
175ml/6fl oz chicken stock
100g/4oz cold unsalted butter, diced
2 shallots, finely chopped
350g/12oz salmon fillet, skinned
salt and freshly ground black pepper
150ml/5floz dry white wine
2 tbsp chopped fresh parsley
a little plain flour
2 eggs, beaten
150g/5oz fresh white breadcrumbs
vegetable oil, for deep-frying
juice of 1 lemon

Cook the potatoes in boiling salted water until tender, then drain and return to the heat to dry out. Remove from the heat and mash. Set aside. Place the stock in a small pan and boil to reduce by two-thirds.

Heat 25g/1oz of the butter in a pan and fry the shallots until softened. Place the salmon on top, season and add the wine and just enough water to cover. Simmer for 5 minutes or until firm but still deep pink in the middle. Remove with a slotted spoon, leave to cool slightly and break into flakes.

Boil the juices remaining in the pan until reduced to about 1 tablespoon. Pour into a bowl, add the salmon, parsley and potatoes, and beat with a wooden spoon until well combined. Season to taste. Roll into 24 small balls, using the palms of your hands. Lightly dust with flour, then dip into the beaten egg and roll in breadcrumbs.

Heat oil to 180°C/350°F or until a cube of bread will brown in 30 seconds. Fry the fish cakes in batches for 4–5 minutes or until golden brown. Drain on kitchen paper and keep warm.

Bring the reduced stock back to the boil. Whisk in the lemon juice and remaining butter, pour into a bowl and serve with the fish cakes.

VINE LEAF PARCELS WITH GOAT'S CHEESE AND OLIVES

You could also barbecue these over medium-hot coals for about the same length of time, making them the perfect garden party canapé.

24 vine leaves in brine, drained
4 tbsp extra-virgin olive oil
350g/12oz goat's cheese
75g/3oz pitted black olives, quartered
salt and freshly ground black pepper

Rinse the vine leaves under cold running water, pat dry on kitchen paper and brush one side of each with oil, using about half of the oil.

Cut the goat's cheese into 24 pieces. Place a piece of cheese and a few olive quarters on each vine leaf. Season well, then roll up the leaves to enclose the filling completely. Secure each parcel with a cocktail stick and brush the parcels with the remaining oil.

Preheat the grill. Grill the parcels for 2–3 minutes on each side or until lightly charred. Serve warm.

Right: Parma Ham and Rocket Crostini

FRENCH-STYLE STUFFED MUSSELS

Many supermarkets now stock fresh, live mussels that have been cleaned, which can save a lot of time. They are at their best from September to April.

24 large live mussels
150ml/5floz dry white wine
2 shallots, finely chopped
juice of 1/2 lemon
75g/3oz butter

2 garlic cloves, crushed
100g/4oz fresh white breadcrumbs
2 tbsp chopped fresh parsley
salt and freshly ground black pepper

Scrub the mussels, remove the beards and rinse well in cold water. Place them in a large pan with the wine and shallots, cover and cook over a high heat for about 5 minutes or until all the mussels are open, shaking the pan frequently. Discard any that do not open. Drain the mussels and remove all the empty half shells. Arrange on a foil-lined grill rack and sprinkle over the lemon juice.

Preheat the grill. Melt the butter in a small pan and fry the garlic for 20 seconds. Remove from the heat and stir in the breadcrumbs, parsley and seasoning. Sprinkle a little of the breadcrumb mixture over each mussel and grill for 1–2 minutes or until lightly browned. Serve hot.

TOASTED POLENTA FINGERS WITH DOLCELATTE SAUCE

This sauce should be served warm, ideally in a small fondue pot or a bowl on a heated serving tray.

200g/7oz polenta
salt and freshly ground black pepper
50g/2oz butter

FOR THE DOLCELATTE SAUCE
1 garlic clove, halved
2 tsp cornflour
2 tbsp lemon juice
75ml/3floz dry white wine
225g/8oz dolcelatte cheese, rind removed

Bring 1.2 litres/2 pints of cold water to the boil in a large pan. Add 1 teaspoon of salt and pour in the polenta in a continuous thin stream, stirring with a wooden spoon. Simmer for about 15 minutes or until the polenta is thickened and no longer grainy, stirring occasionally.

Remove the pan from the heat and stir in half the butter. Season with pepper. Turn out on to a wooden board and spread out to 1cm/1/2in thickness. Leave to cool, then cover and chill for at least 1 hour.

Preheat the grill. Cut the set polenta into 24 diamond shapes, each about 4cm/11/2in long, and place on a foil-lined grill rack. Melt the remaining butter and brush over both sides of the polenta shapes. Grill for 3–4 minutes on each side. Cover loosely and keep warm.

To make the sauce, rub the garlic around the inside of a small heavy-based pan (then discard the garlic). Blend the cornflour to a paste with the lemon juice. Put the wine in the pan with the blended cornflour, crumble in the dolcelatte and slowly bring to the boil, stirring all the time. Simmer gently for 5 minutes, stirring frequently. Season with pepper. Serve warm, with the toasted polenta fingers for dipping.

CHEESE AND OLIVE SABLÉ SHAPES

Instead of the olives, you could decorate these biscuits with chopped sun-dried tomatoes that have been preserved in oil or small pieces of anchovy fillet. Pack the shapes into a rigid container to freeze for up to 1 month. To use, defrost thoroughly on baking trays and crisp up in a hot oven. Makes about 20.

50g/2oz small pitted black olives, halved

FOR THE DOUGH
75g/3oz plain flour, plus extra for dusting
50g/2oz chilled butter, cubed

50g/2oz Parmesan, freshly grated
1 egg, beaten

Preheat the oven to 180°C/350°F/Gas 4. Sift the flour into a bowl and rub in the butter until the mixture resembles fine breadcrumbs. Stir in the Parmesan with 1 tablespoon of chilled water and mix to a firm dough.

Knead the dough briefly and roll out thinly on a lightly floured surface. Stamp out star and moon shapes and arrange on a baking tray. Brush with the beaten egg and press half an olive into the middle of each one. Bake for 10–12 minutes or until crisp and golden brown. Leave to cool on a wire rack before serving.

CHICKEN LIVER PÂTÉ TOASTS WITH ONION CONSERVE

You need to make this quantity of pâté because less will not blend properly in the food processor. You can prepare the pâté and conserve up to 24 hours in advance; cover and chill until needed. Makes 48.

25g/1oz unsalted butter
225g/8oz chicken livers, thawed if frozen
1 small garlic clove, crushed
1/2 tsp chopped fresh marjoram
2 tbsp brandy
12 slices white bread

FOR THE ONION CONSERVE
25g/1oz butter
2 onions, thinly sliced
25g/1oz sugar
3 tbsp redcurrant jelly
2 tbsp red wine vinegar
150ml/5floz red wine
salt and freshly ground black pepper

Melt half the butter in a pan and gently fry the chicken livers, garlic and marjoram for about 10 minutes, stirring occasionally. Stir in the brandy and remove from the heat. Leave to cool slightly. Place the mixture in a food processor and blend until smooth. Spoon into a small dish and chill for at least 2 hours or until firm.

To make the onion conserve: melt the butter in a pan, add the onions and cook over a low heat, uncovered, for about 30 minutes, stirring frequently. Add the sugar, redcurrant jelly, vinegar and wine and cook gently for a further 20 minutes or until thickened. Season to taste.

Toast the bread and stamp out four rounds from each slice, using a 5cm/2in metal cutter. Leave to cool on a wire rack.

To serve, spread each toast round thickly with some of the chicken liver pâté and place a little of the onion conserve on top.

Right: French-Style Stuffed Mussels

QUICK & EASY

These days, who wants to be stuck in the kitchen for hours preparing food? The recipes in this chapter have been devised with the busy cook in mind – all of them can be made in less than half an hour. The ingredients needed have been kept to a minimum, and many of them will be found in a well-stocked storecupboard. Look at the suggestions on pages 9–11 and tailor them to suit your needs. All recipes serve 4.

SWEETCORN FRITTERS WITH SWEET CHILLI SAUCE

These are extremely simple to make and you could add all sorts of flavourings to the fritters, such as some crushed garlic and ginger and finely chopped red chilli. But they taste wonderful just as they are, dipped into a little sweet chilli sauce.

200g/7oz can sweetcorn, drained
3 tbsp plain flour
1 tsp baking powder
1 tsp hot chilli powder
1 egg
salt and freshly ground black pepper
vegetable oil, for frying
120ml/4floz sweet chilli sauce

Place the sweetcorn, flour, baking powder, chilli powder and egg in a bowl and mix until well combined. Season generously.

Heat 2.5cm/1in of oil in a deep frying pan. Put five or six heaped tablespoons of the batter into the pan and flatten slightly with a fork. Fry for about 5 minutes, turning once, until crisp and golden brown. Drain on kitchen paper. Keep each batch warm while frying the remainder. Serve hot, with the chilli sauce.

FRITTO MISTO

You can vary the fish you use for this recipe, depending on what is available. Cod, haddock or sole would all work well for the white fish fillets or you could substitute 5mm/1/4in squid rings.

225g/8oz firm white fish fillets, skinned
4 small red mullet, cleaned and filleted
12 raw tiger or king prawns
2 tbsp seasoned flour
vegetable oil, for deep-frying
lemon wedges, to garnish

Cut the white fish fillets into long thin strips, and slice the red mullet fillets. Peel the prawns, leaving their tails intact. Place the seasoned flour on a plate and toss in all the fish to coat.

Heat oil to 190°C/375°F or until a cube of bread will brown in 20 seconds. Add the fish pieces a few at a time and fry until golden brown. Drain on kitchen paper. Keep each batch warm while frying the remainder. Arrange on a serving platter, garnish with the lemon wedges and serve.

GARLIC PITTA FINGERS WITH TARAMASALATA

Pitta bread is the ideal standby as it can be grilled from frozen, so it's always worth having a packet tucked away in your freezer.

50g/2oz butter
2 garlic cloves, crushed
1 tbsp chopped fresh herbs, such as oregano and parsley
salt and freshly ground black pepper
8 white pitta breads
150g/5oz carton taramasalata

Preheat the grill. Melt the butter in a small pan and stir in the garlic, herbs and seasoning. Arrange the pitta breads on a grill rack and grill for 1 minute.

Turn the pitta breads over and brush liberally with the garlic butter. Grill for another 1–2 minutes, then cut into strips. Serve at once with the taramasalata.

Above: Melted Cheese and Sweetcorn Nachos

SWEET POTATO FRITTERS WITH BLUE CHEESE DIP

These crisp Parmesan-coated potato fritters are perfectly complemented by the blue cheese and yoghurt dip.

450g/1lb sweet potatoes	*25g/1oz Parmesan, grated*
1 tbsp seasoned flour	*sunflower oil, for deep-frying*
1 egg	*75g/3oz soft blue cheese, crumbled*
salt and freshly ground black pepper	*4 tbsp Greek yoghurt*
75g/3oz dried white breadcrumbs	

Peel the sweet potatoes and cut into sticks. Coat in the seasoned flour. Beat the egg with 2 tablespoons of water and season well. Mix the breadcrumbs, Parmesan and seasoning on a plate. Coat the sweet potato sticks in the beaten egg and then in the breadcrumb mixture.

Heat oil to 180°C/350°F or until a cube of bread will brown in 30 seconds. While the oil is heating, mash the blue cheese in a small bowl and gradually beat in the yoghurt. Season to taste and set aside.

Fry the sweet potato sticks in batches for 3–4 minutes or until crisp and golden. Drain on kitchen paper and serve at once, with the dip.

SAUSAGE AND HERB NUGGETS WITH APRICOT RELISH

It's worth buying good-quality sausages for this recipe. You can use any combination of herbs you like: parsley, sage and thyme work very well with pork sausages.

400g/14oz can apricot halves in syrup	*450g/1lb butcher's sausages*
3 tbsp sunflower oil	*2 tbsp chopped fresh herbs, such as*
1 onion, finely chopped	*thyme, sage and parsley*
2 tbsp white wine vinegar	*2 tbsp seasoned flour*
2 tsp mustard seeds	

To make the apricot relish, drain the apricots, reserving 6 tablespoons of the juice, and chop into small pieces. Heat 1 tablespoon of the oil in a pan and fry the onion until softened. Add the apricots, reserved juice, vinegar and mustard seeds and simmer for about 15 minutes or until well reduced and thickened.

Squeeze the sausage meat out of the skins and knead with the herbs and 4 tablespoons of the apricot relish. Divide into 20 pieces and roll each one into a ball with wet hands. Dust the balls lightly with the sesasoned flour.

Heat the remaining oil in a large frying pan and fry the nuggets for about 10 minutes or until lightly golden, turning occasionally. Drain on kitchen paper and place on a serving platter. Serve hot, with the rest of the apricot relish in a small bowl for dipping.

MELTED CHEESE AND SWEETCORN NACHOS

This literally takes minutes to make. You can also use frozen sweetcorn, which needs to be thawed before use. Or if fresh sweetcorn is in season, scrape the kernels from the cob and cook them in a little water for about 5 minutes or until just tender.

225g/8oz packet tortilla chips	*4 tbsp soured cream*
100g/4oz can sweetcorn, drained	*salt and freshly ground black pepper*
2 tomatoes, chopped	*50g/2oz Cheddar cheese, grated*
4 spring onions, chopped	

Preheat the grill. Spread the tortilla chips in a large, shallow oven dish and scatter the sweetcorn, tomatoes and spring onions on top. Spoon over the soured cream, season to taste and sprinkle over the Cheddar.

Grill for 2–3 minutes or until the cheese has melted and is bubbling. Serve at once.

QUICK MOZZARELLA AND SALAMI PIZZAS

To make this recipe even faster, you could use a 225g/8oz jar of pasta tomato sauce with herbs for the tomato base.

3 tbsp olive oil
1 small onion, finely chopped
400g/14oz can chopped tomatoes
1 tbsp tomato purée
1 tsp dried mixed herbs

salt and freshly ground black pepper
4 English muffins
150g/5oz salami, sliced
225g/8oz mozzarella cheese, sliced

Heat half the oil in a small pan and fry the onion until softened. Stir in the tomatoes, tomato purée, herbs and seasoning and simmer for 5–10 minutes or until reduced and thickened slightly.

Preheat the grill. Split the muffins in half horizontally and spread some of the tomato mixture on the cut surface of each half. Cut the salami slices into quarters, if large, and scatter over the pizza bases. Arrange the mozzarella on top and drizzle over the remaining oil. Grill for about 5 minutes or until bubbling and golden. Serve at once.

FRIED AUBERGINES WITH SKORDALIA

This is a very traditional Greek dish that is often served as part of a meze (a selection of nibbles) in restaurants. You need to serve it immediately or the aubergine will start to soften.

olive oil, for frying
450g/1lb large aubergine, thinly sliced
2 tbsp seasoned flour

FOR THE SKORDALIA
100g/4oz slightly stale white breadcrumbs
175ml/6fl oz milk
2 garlic cloves, crushed

1 tbsp white wine vinegar
150ml/5fl oz extra-virgin olive oil
salt and freshly ground black pepper

To make the skordalia, place the breadcrumbs and milk in a bowl and leave to soak for 10 minutes. Whisk in the garlic and vinegar, then slowly pour in the olive oil in a thin stream, whisking constantly. Season to taste and set aside.

Pour enough olive oil into a deep frying pan to make a 1cm/^{1}/2in depth. Heat the oil to 190°C/375°F or until a cube of bread will brown in 20 seconds. Dip the aubergine slices in the seasoned flour and fry in batches for 1–2 minutes or until golden brown. Drain on kitchen paper and keep warm while frying the remainder.

Arrange the fried aubergine on serving plates with the skordalia on the side and serve at once.

CRISPY MUSHROOMS WITH GOAT'S CHEESE MAYONNAISE

This is not really a mayonnaise in the true sense of the word, but actually tastes even better! You can buy tubs of soft goat's cheese, which has a similar texture to full fat creamy cheese, from the chilled cabinets in the supermarket.

225g/8oz soft goat's cheese
4 tbsp soured cream
2 tbsp snipped fresh chives
450g/1lb mixed mushrooms, such as chestnut, field or button

2 eggs
salt and freshly ground black pepper
75g/3oz dried breadcrumbs
vegetable oil, for deep-frying
1 tbsp lemon juice

Place the goat's cheese in a bowl and beat with a wooden spoon until smooth. Beat in the soured cream and chives until well combined. Taste and add a little seasoning if necessary, then spoon into a small serving bowl.

Cut the large mushrooms into bite-sized pieces – the smaller ones can be left whole. Beat the eggs in a bowl and season well. Dip the mushrooms first into the beaten egg and then into the breadcrumbs to coat completely.

Heat oil to 180°C/350°F or until a cube of bread will brown in 30 seconds. Fry the mushrooms in batches for 1–2 minutes or until crisp and golden. Drain on kitchen paper, sprinkle over the lemon juice and serve at once, with the goat's cheese mayonnaise.

Above: Quick Mozzarella and Salami Pizzas

CRISPY NEW POTATOES WITH MUSTARD RELISH

These potatoes are absolutely delicious just on their own, but the mustard relish is an excellent extra. It is available in jars from most major supermarkets and shops.

450g/1lb baby new potatoes (about 20)
10 smoked streaky bacon rashers
3 tbsp olive oil
1 tbsp chopped fresh thyme

2 garlic cloves, finely chopped
salt and freshly ground black pepper
100g/4oz mustard relish

Preheat the oven to 200°C/400°F/Gas 6. Place the potatoes in a pan of boiling salted water and simmer for 10–15 minutes or until just tender. Meanwhile, cut each bacon rasher in half lengthways. Place the oil, thyme, garlic and seasoning in a bowl.

When the potatoes are done, drain and tip into the oil mixture, turning to coat. Wrap a piece of bacon around each potato and arrange in a small roasting tin. Drizzle over the remaining oil mixture and bake for 15–20 minutes or until crisp. Spoon the mustard relish into a small bowl and serve with the potatoes.

MOZZARELLA FRITTERS WITH A SPICY TOMATO SAUCE

Traditional Italian mozzarella is creamy white and normally sold in ball shapes. The Danish version is slightly yellow and comes in block form, making it easier to slice.

400g/14oz can chopped tomatoes
4 tbsp sweet chilli sauce
1/2 tsp cayenne pepper
salt and freshly ground black pepper
350g/12oz Danish mozzarella cheese

100g/4oz fine fresh white breadcrumbs
2 tbsp chopped fresh parsley
2 eggs
vegetable oil, for deep-frying

Place the tomatoes, chilli sauce, half the cayenne and a little seasoning in a small pan. Bring to the boil, reduce the heat and simmer gently for 15–20 minutes or until well reduced and thickened.

Meanwhile, cut the mozzarella into 12 rectangular slices, each about 2.5 x 7.5cm/1 x 3in. Mix together the breadcrumbs, parsley, remaining cayenne pepper and seasoning in a bowl. Lightly beat the eggs in a small bowl. Dip the mozzarella slices first into the beaten egg and then into the breadcrumb mixture. Repeat the process, dipping them carefully the second time.

Heat oil to 190°C/375°F or until a cube of bread will brown in 20 seconds. Deep-fry the mozzarella slices in batches for about 2 minutes or until crisp and golden. Drain on kitchen paper and serve hot, with the warm sauce.

BAGNA CAUDA

This is a very potent garlic dip that can be eaten with bread and all manner of raw vegetables – instead of carrots and radishes you could try cauliflower florets, sliced peppers or courgette sticks. Keep the dip warm over a food warmer or in a fondue pot, if you have one.

50g/2oz unsalted butter
120ml/4fl oz extra-virgin olive oil
2 large garlic cloves, crushed
50g/2oz can anchovy fillets, drained

freshly ground black pepper
2 large carrots, cut into sticks
100g/4oz radishes
225g/8oz Italian-style bread, cut into chunks

Melt the butter in a pan with the oil and stir in the garlic and anchovies. Cook over a very low heat for 10–15 minutes, stirring frequently. Season with pepper.

Serve warm with the vegetables and bread.

Right: Crispy New Potatoes with Mustard Relish

Swiss Cheese Fondue

Don't worry if you haven't got a fondue set. You can make this in a small heavy-based pan and keep it hot over a food warmer for serving.

1 large garlic clove, halved
2 tsp cornflour
2 tbsp Kirsch
225g/8oz Emmental cheese, grated

100g/4oz Gruyère cheese, grated
250ml/8fl oz dry white wine
freshly ground black pepper
1 large French stick, cut into chunks

Rub the inside of the fondue pan with the cut surface of the garlic; discard the garlic. Blend the cornflour to a paste with the Kirsch and place in the pan with the cheeses and wine. Bring slowly to the boil, stirring continuously.

Reduce the heat and simmer gently for 3–4 minutes, stirring frequently. Season to taste with the pepper. Place the pan over the fondue burner at the table. Serve with the bread for dipping.

Vegetable Crisps with Soured Cream Dip

These have become very trendy and can be seen in some of the best restaurants. They taste wonderful and are much more colourful than normal potato crisps, so try making your own.

1 parsnip
1 large carrot
1 cooked beetroot
vegetable oil, for frying

150ml/5floz soured cream
2 tbsp snipped fresh chives
salt and freshly ground black pepper

Using a vegetable peeler or sharp knife, cut the vegetables into very thin slices. Pat dry with kitchen paper to remove any excess moisture.

Heat about 2.5cm/1in of oil in a deep frying pan and fry the vegetables in batches for 1–2 minutes or until golden. Remove with a slotted spoon and drain on kitchen paper. When all the vegetables are done, season well and arrange on a serving platter.

Mix together the soured cream and chives, season to taste and serve in a small bowl, with the vegetable crisps.

Spanish Omelette Wedges

Remember to protect your frying pan handle with doubled foil, if necessary, when grilling. You can use older spinach leaves; just remove all the thick stalks and any damaged bits, then tear into small pieces.

4 tbsp olive oil
225g/8oz onions, sliced
450g/1lb potatoes, thinly sliced
225g/8oz young tender spinach leaves

50g/2oz Gruyère cheese, grated
6 eggs
salt and freshly ground black pepper

Heat the oil in a 20cm/8in frying pan and gently fry the onions for about 10 minutes or until softened. Meanwhile, blanch the potato slices in a pan of boiling salted water for 3 minutes. Drain and pat dry.

Add the potatoes to the pan with the onions and cook for a further 5 minutes or until the potatoes are lightly golden, stirring frequently. Stir in the spinach leaves and cook for 1–2 minutes or until just wilted. Sprinkle the cheese on top.

Preheat the grill. Whisk the eggs in a bowl with plenty of seasoning, then pour over the potato and onion mixture, pressing down gently. Cook for another 5 minutes or until the top is nearly set, then place under the hot grill for 2–3 minutes or until golden brown. Cut into eight wedges and serve either warm or cold.

Sizzling Chorizo and Cherry Tomato Skewers

If you can get hold of a mixture of red and yellow cherry tomatoes, these skewers really look great. Chorizo is a Spanish sausage and is made from pork and lots of paprika, which gives it a distinctive bright red colour.

3 tbsp sun-dried tomato paste
1 garlic clove, crushed
1/2 tsp chilli powder

1 tbsp honey
350g/12oz chorizo sausage, sliced
225g/8oz cherry tomatoes

Preheat the grill. In a small bowl, mix together the sun-dried tomato paste, garlic, chilli powder and honey to a thick paste. Thread the slices of chorizo and cherry tomatoes alternately on to eight 15cm/6in bamboo skewers.

Using a pastry brush, spread the sun-dried tomato mixture all over the skewers to give a good coating. Grill for 1–2 minutes on each side or until the chorizo is heated through and sizzling. Serve at once.

Right: Vegetable Crisps with Soured Cream Dip

STEAMED BABY VEGETABLES WITH HOLLANDAISE

A wonderful selection of baby vegetables is now available. Not only do they look great, but they also have a delicate, sweet flavour.

2 whole eggs and 1 egg yolk
1 tbsp lemon juice
good pinch of salt
225g/8oz unsalted butter

450g/1lb mixed baby vegetables, such as carrots, sweetcorn, leeks, courgettes and mangetouts
1 tbsp chopped fresh tarragon

Put the eggs and egg yolk, lemon juice and salt into a food processor and blend for 10 seconds. Melt the butter in a small pan until it just begins to foam, but not burn. Then, with the food processor running, pour the butter on to the egg mixture in a continuous thin stream. Pour the resulting sauce into the pan and heat gently, stirring frequently, for about 30 seconds or until thickened. This hollandaise sauce will keep for 10 minutes set over another pan of warm water.

Steam the baby vegetables for 4–5 minutes or until just tender. Pour the hollandaise sauce into a bowl, stir in the tarragon and place in the middle of a warmed serving platter. Arrange the vegetables around it and serve at once.

COURGETTE FRITTERS WITH RED PESTO SAUCE

Red pesto sauce gets its colour from sun-dried tomatoes. If you prefer, you could use the more widely available green pesto sauce.

150g/5oz plain flour
salt and freshly ground black pepper
2 eggs, separated
200ml/7fl oz light ale
2 tbsp vegetable oil, plus extra for deep-frying

200g/7oz can chopped tomatoes
4 tbsp red pesto sauce
450g/1lb small courgettes, cut into thick slices

To make the batter, sift the flour and 1 teaspoon of salt into a bowl and make a well in the centre. Gradually beat in the egg yolks, light ale, the oil and seasoning to make a smooth batter.

Mix the tomatoes and pesto sauce in a small pan. Season to taste and simmer for about 5 minutes or until thickened slightly. Keep warm.

Heat oil to 180°C/350°F or until a cube of bread will brown in 30 seconds. Whisk the egg whites until stiff and fold into the batter. Dip the courgette slices into the batter a few at a time and fry in batches for 2–3 minutes or until crisp and golden. Drain on kitchen paper and keep warm while frying the remainder. Serve hot, with the sauce.

GRILLED SQUID WITH FETA

Squid has the undeserved reputation of being tough and rubbery. It is perfectly tender if cooked either very quickly, as in this recipe, or very slowly. Look out for ready-prepared squid in the fishmongers if you don't want to clean it yourself.

8 small squid, about 450g/1lb in total
4 tbsp extra-virgin olive oil
2 tbsp lemon juice
1 garlic clove, crushed

2 tsp chopped fresh flat-leaf parsley
salt and freshly ground black pepper
175g/6oz feta cheese, cubed

To prepare the squid, hold the body firmly in one hand, grip the head and tentacles with the other hand, and pull gently; they will come away along with the contents of the body.

Cut off the tentacles, just in front of the eyes, and remove the ink sac. Peel off the thin layer of skin that covers the body and discard. Pull out the plastic-like quill. Rinse the squid well under cold running water.

Mix together the olive oil, lemon juice, garlic, parsley and seasoning in a shallow non-metallic dish. Add the squid and feta and turn to coat. Set aside for 15 minutes.

Preheat the grill. Remove the squid from the marinade and stuff each cavity with feta. Arrange on a rack in a foil-lined grill pan and brush with any remaining marinade. Grill for 5 minutes on each side or until cooked through and lightly browned. Serve hot.

GARLIC AND LEMON MUSHROOMS

Field mushrooms always have a superb flavour as they have been left to mature completely. Some people peel off the skins, but unless they are very ragged or bruised, you really need not bother.

8 large flat field mushrooms, each about 10cm/4in across
2 large garlic cloves, crushed
grated rind and juice of 1 lemon

6 tbsp olive oil
salt and freshly ground black pepper
2 tbsp chopped fresh flat-leaf parsley
warm French bread, to serve

Preheat the oven to 200°C/400°F/Gas 6. Trim the stalks off the mushrooms. Arrange the mushrooms, stalk side up, in a shallow roasting tin.

Mix together the garlic, lemon rind and juice, oil and seasoning in a small bowl. Drizzle the oil mixture over the mushrooms and bake for 15 minutes. Turn the mushrooms over, baste well with the oil mixture in the tin and bake for a further 5–10 minutes or until tender.

Arrange the mushrooms on serving plates, scatter over the parsley and serve at once, with French bread to mop up all the juices.

Right: Steamed Baby Vegetables with Hollandaise

LIGHT & HEALTHY

Contrary to popular belief, casual eating does not have to be unhealthy and bad for you. The recipes here prove this point perfectly. Coming home late after an evening out, a full-scale dinner is often out of the question, but a light and wholesome snack can just fit the bill. You can also use these recipes for entertaining: as nibbles, first courses, or for buffets.

TURKEY AND CHERRY TOMATO TWISTS

Turkey joints are now widely available in supermarkets. They are low in fat and often cheaper than chicken. Makes 24.

3 tbsp plain yoghurt
1 small garlic clove, crushed
1 tsp grated root ginger
grated rind of 1 lime

1 tbsp clear honey
salt and freshly ground black pepper
450g/1lb turkey breast fillets, skinned
175g/6oz tiny cherry tomatoes

Place the yoghurt, garlic, ginger, lime rind, honey and seasoning in a non-metallic bowl. Slice the turkey into 24 strips, each about 15 x 1cm/6 x 1/2in. Place in the marinade and turn to coat. Cover and chill for at least 30 minutes or overnight.

Preheat the grill. Thread each turkey strip on to a 15cm/6in bamboo skewer, interweaving with the cherry tomatoes. Grill for 8–10 minutes, turning occasionally, until the turkey is cooked through. Serve hot.

ASPARAGUS WITH CRAB DIP

Try to use good-quality crab for this recipe. Fresh is ideal, but thawed, frozen crab would also be fine. Serves 4–6.

675g/1 1/2lb asparagus spears

FOR THE CRAB DIP
225g/8oz white crab meat, flaked
25g/1oz butter, melted
100g/4oz cream cheese
4 tbsp plain yoghurt

juice of 1/2 lemon
2 tbsp snipped fresh chives
freshly ground black pepper

Trim any woody ends from the asparagus and discard. Trim all the spears to the same length and divide into four equal bundles. Secure each bundle with string, under the tips and near the base.

Stand the bundles in an asparagus steamer or deep pan. Add enough boiling salted water to come half way up the stalks. Bring to the boil, then cover with a lid or dome of foil and simmer for 8–10 minutes or until the bases of the stalks are just tender when pierced with a knife.

Meanwhile, make the dip: mix all the ingredients together in a bowl with a fork or in a food processor. Pour the mixture into a serving dish.

Drain the cooked asparagus thoroughly, remove the string and arrange on a serving platter with the dip. Serve at once.

PERSIAN GRILLED BABY AUBERGINES

If you can't get baby aubergines, use three medium ones and cut them lengthways into slices. Serves 4.

75g/3oz creamed coconut, crumbled
2 garlic cloves, crushed
1 red chilli, seeded and finely chopped
grated rind of 1 small lemon

1 tsp ground cumin
2 tbsp chopped fresh coriander
10 baby aubergines
1 tsp salt

Place the coconut in a small pan, pour in 175ml/6floz of boiling water and stir until smooth. Add the garlic, chilli, lemon rind, cumin and coriander and simmer for 5–10 minutes or until thickened to a paste. Leave to cool.

Meanwhile, halve the aubergines and sprinkle with the salt. Leave in a colander to drain for 30 minutes, then rinse under cold running water and pat dry with kitchen paper.

Preheat the grill. Spread the coconut paste all over the cut surfaces of the aubergine halves and grill for 15–20 minutes or until cooked through and lightly charred. Serve at once.

FALAFEL WITH YOGHURT MINT RELISH

This Middle Eastern recipe is normally deep-fried. However, it is just as successful made this way and has fewer calories. Makes 24.

400g/14oz can chickpeas, drained
and rinsed
1 large garlic clove, crushed
1/2 tsp each ground coriander and cumin
1 egg yolk
50g/2oz fresh white breadcrumbs
2 tbsp olive oil

FOR THE YOGHURT MINT RELISH
150ml/5floz Greek yoghurt
50g/2oz cucumber, grated and squeezed dry
1 tsp mint sauce

To make the relish, mix together the yoghurt, cucumber and mint sauce in a small bowl. Cover and chill until needed.

Place the chickpeas, garlic, spices and egg yolk in a food processor and blend until smooth. Stir in the breadcrumbs.

Divide the falafel mixture into 24 pieces. Roll into balls and flatten slightly. Heat the olive oil in a heavy-based frying pan, add the falafel and fry for 6–8 minutes or until golden brown all over. Serve at once, with the yoghurt mint relish for dipping.

HONEY-GLAZED CHICKEN TIKKA SKEWERS

Tikka curry paste is now widely available. The honey glaze makes the skewers glisten invitingly. Makes 24.

450g/1lb boneless chicken breast, skinned
4 tbsp plain yoghurt
2 garlic cloves, crushed
2.5cm/1in piece root ginger, crushed
1/2 tsp salt

1 tbsp tikka curry paste
3 tbsp clear honey
1 tbsp lemon juice
1 tbsp finely chopped fresh mint

Cut the chicken into 1cm/1/2in cubes. Mix together the yoghurt, garlic, ginger, salt and tikka paste in a bowl and stir in the chicken cubes. Leave to marinate for at least 30 minutes and up to 12 hours.

Preheat the grill. Thread the marinated chicken on to 24 cocktail sticks and grill for 2–3 minutes on each side.

Meanwhile, warm the honey and lemon juice together in a small pan. Brush all over each skewer, sprinkle over the mint and serve at once.

POTATO SKINS WITH AVOCADO AND RED ONION SALSA

You can prepare this in advance. Brush the potato skins with oil and make the salsa, then cover both and chill for up to 24 hours. When ready to serve, bake the potato skins in a preheated 200°C/400°F/ Gas 6 oven for about 15 minutes or until golden. Serves 4.

6 potatoes, each about 100g/4oz
2 tbsp sunflower oil

FOR THE AVOCADO AND RED ONION SALSA
225g/8oz ripe tomatoes, diced
1 ripe avocado, diced
1 small red onion, finely chopped

2 tbsp chilli sauce
salt and freshly ground black pepper

Preheat the oven to 200°C/400°F/Gas 6. Scrub the potatoes and dry them well with kitchen paper. Rub each potato with a little of the oil and place them directly on the oven shelf. Bake for 40–45 minutes or until the potatoes are slightly softened when squeezed.

Meanwhile, make the salsa: mix together the tomatoes, avocado, onion and chilli sauce in a small bowl. Season to taste. Cover with cling film and chill until needed.

When the potatoes are tender, remove them from the oven and cut them in half lengthways and then into quarters. Slice away some of the flesh, leaving a layer of potato at least 1cm/1/2in thick on the skin.

Preheat the grill. Spread the potato skins on baking trays, brush lightly with the remaining oil and grill for 5–10 minutes or until crisp and golden brown. Arrange the potato skins on a serving plate with the salsa, sprinkle with a little salt and serve.

Above: Honey-Glazed Chicken Tikka Skewers

DUBLIN BAY PRAWNS WITH TRICOLOUR DIP

If you cannot find Dublin Bay prawns, sometimes called langoustines, use large Mediterranean prawns. It is important that the prawns are very fresh, otherwise they may have lost both texture and flavour. Makes 24.

24 fresh raw Dublin Bay prawns

FOR THE TRICOLOUR DIP
1 large orange pepper, seeded and
quartered
6 tbsp Greek yoghurt
2 tbsp soured cream

1 small garlic clove, crushed
1–2 tsp lemon juice
salt and freshly ground black pepper
2 tsp snipped fresh chives

Rinse the prawns in cold water. Place in a large pan of boiling water, return to the boil and poach for 3 minutes. Drain, refresh quickly under cold running water and leave to cool. You can shell them now, leaving the tails intact, or leave them for your guests to shell.

To make the dip, preheat the grill and grill the pepper until the skin is charred. Wrap in cling film and leave to cool, then peel off the skin. Purée the pepper flesh in a food processor or blender.

Put the yoghurt, soured cream, garlic, lemon juice and seasoning in a bowl and mix well. Spoon into a serving bowl and swirl in the pepper purée, using a thin metal skewer. Sprinkle the chives in a small heap in the middle of the dip, and serve with the prawns.

MARINATED GREEK OLIVES

Although these olives are preserved in oil, once they are drained there is hardly any oil left on them. They can also be used in cocktails. Makes 500g/1¼ pints.

450g/1lb large green olives
4 small garlic cloves, peeled
pared rind of 1 lemon
6 small dried red chillies

2 sprigs each fresh thyme and oregano
1 tsp fennel seeds
olive oil, for filling

Using the tip of a sharp knife, cut a slit in each olive through to the stone. Layer the olives with the garlic, lemon rind, chillies, herb sprigs and fennel seeds in a 500g/1¼ pint glass jar.

Pour in enough oil to cover the olives completely, then close the jar and leave for at least 1 week and up to 1 month before using.

TABBOULEH PARTY PITTA POCKETS

These make the perfect calorie-conscious canapés. However, you could use the mixture to stuff warmed mini pitta breads for a healthy snack. Makes 24.

100g/4oz bulgar wheat
juice of 1 large lemon
1 small garlic clove, crushed
2 tbsp each chopped fresh mint and parsley
½ tsp ground cumin

2 tomatoes, peeled, seeded and diced
4 spring onions, finely chopped
100g/4oz feta cheese, finely chopped
24 party pitta pockets

Soak the bulgar wheat in a large bowl of cold water for 30 minutes; drain thoroughly. Blend the lemon juice, garlic, mint, parsley and cumin in a small bowl and stir into the bulgar wheat. Leave to marinate for at least 30 minutes and up to 8 hours.

Add the tomatoes, spring onions and feta cheese and mix well.

Lightly toast the pitta pockets and split each one across the top. Stuff with the tabbouleh and serve.

MIXED MUSHROOM BASKETS

Make sure you don't allow the fromage frais to come to the boil or it will curdle and separate, because of its low fat content. Serves 4.

4 round white bread rolls
40g/1½oz butter
1 onion, finely chopped
275g/10oz mixed mushrooms, such as oyster, shiitake and chestnut, sliced if large

1 tbsp Madeira
6 tbsp low-fat fromage frais
2 tsp snipped fresh chives
salt and freshly ground black pepper

Preheat the oven to 200°C/400°F/Gas 6. Cut the tops off the rolls and scoop out the middles, leaving a 1cm/½in shell. Melt half the butter and brush inside the rolls. Bake for 8–10 minutes or until golden.

Melt the remaining butter in a pan and fry the onion until softened. Add the mushrooms and fry for about 5 minutes. Sprinkle over the Madeira and stir in the fromage frais and chives. Cook for 1–2 minutes, until heated through. Season to taste, spoon into the rolls and serve hot.

MINI SEAFOOD BROCHETTES WITH MANGO MASH

You could use canned coconut milk in this recipe, but it's more economical to make small quantities from a block of creamed coconut. Crumble 40g/1½oz creamed coconut into a heatproof jug and pour in boiling water to make up to 150ml/5floz, stirring continuously until smooth. Serves 4.

225g/8oz monkfish fillet, skinned and cut into 8 chunks
8 raw tiger or king prawns, shelled, leaving tail intact
8 queen scallops

FOR THE MANGO MASH
150ml/5floz coconut milk
1 garlic clove, crushed
1 small green chilli, seeded and finely chopped

1 mango, peeled and chopped
juice of 1 lime
2 tbsp chopped fresh coriander
salt and freshly ground black pepper

To make the mango mash, place the coconut milk in a pan with the garlic and chilli and simmer for 10 minutes. Leave to cool, then transfer to a food processor. Add the mango, lime juice and coriander and whizz until blended. Season to taste and pour into a serving bowl.

Preheat the grill. Thread the monkfish, prawns and scallops on to eight 15cm/6in bamboo skewers. Season and place on a lightly oiled grill rack. Grill for 8–10 minutes, turning occasionally, until cooked and lightly browned. Serve at once, with the mango mash.

Above: Mini Seafood Brochettes with Mango Mash

NIÇOISE PLATTER WITH GARLIC YOGHURT

This is a variation of the classic salad and looks striking with its combination of strong colours. You could serve it with garlic toast, made by baking or grilling small slices of rustic-style bread that have been rubbed with a halved garlic clove and drizzled with oil. Serves 4.

225g/8oz French beans, trimmed
2 eggs
100g/4oz radishes
2 ripe plum tomatoes
50g/2oz pitted black olives

juice of 1 small lemon
150ml/5floz Greek yoghurt
10cm/4in piece cucumber, seeded and diced
1 garlic clove, crushed
salt and freshly ground black pepper

Add the French beans to a pan of boiling salted water and simmer for 3 minutes. Drain and refresh in cold running water. Bring another small pan of water to the boil, add the eggs, return to the boil and simmer gently for 7 minutes. Drain and cool under cold running water, then peel and cut in half.

Trim the radishes and cut in half if large. Cut the plum tomatoes into quarters. Arrange the beans, eggs, radishes, tomatoes and olives on a serving platter, sprinkle over the lemon juice and season to taste.

To make the garlic yoghurt, mix together the yoghurt, cucumber and garlic in a small serving bowl and season well. Place on the platter and use as a dip.

MEDITERRANEAN VEGETABLE PLATTER WITH SALSA VERDE

You can make your own sun-dried tomato paste with a jar of sun-dried tomatoes preserved in oil. Tip the tomatoes and oil into a food processor, blend until smooth, then pack back into the jar. Serves 4.

2 tbsp olive oil
1 garlic clove, crushed
2 tbsp sun-dried tomato paste
1 small aubergine, cut into
5cm/2in thick slices
1 small red and 1 small yellow pepper,
seeded and cut into quarters
2 small courgettes, cut in half lengthways

FOR THE SALSA VERDE
2 large plum tomatoes, peeled, seeded
and diced
1 green chilli, seeded and finely chopped
2 tbsp chopped fresh coriander
juice of 1 lime

Mix together the oil, garlic and sun-dried tomato paste in a small bowl. Place the vegetables in a shallow non-metallic dish and brush with the paste. Cover and leave to marinate for 30 minutes.

Make the salsa verde: mix together the tomatoes, chilli, coriander and lime juice in a small serving bowl and set aside at room temperature.

Preheat the grill. Arrange the vegetables on a grill rack and grill for 10–15 minutes, turning occasionally, until cooked through and slightly charred. Serve at once, with the salsa verde.

PICKLED HERRING AND MUSTARD TOASTS

This is a good storecupboard standby as you can buy the pickled herrings in jars. They are low in fat and quite delicious. Makes 24.

5 slices brown bread
4 pickled herring fillets
2 tbsp wholegrain mustard

150ml/5floz Greek yoghurt
salt and freshly ground black pepper
24 tiny dill sprigs

Preheat the grill. Using a 4cm/1½in fluted pastry cutter, stamp out 24 rounds from the bread. Place on a grill rack and lightly toast on both sides. Leave to cool on a wire rack.

Cut the herring into 24 pieces, each about 2.5cm/1in. Mix together the mustard, yoghurt and seasoning and spread over the toasts. Top each toast with a piece of herring and a dill sprig. Serve at once.

PROSCIUTTO AND MELON SKEWERS

This classic combination looks good threaded on to small skewers or cocktail sticks. There is no cooking required. Makes 24.

12 thin slices prosciutto
1 large ripe melon, such as cantaloupe
24 small mint leaves

Cut each slice of prosciutto in half lengthways. Cut the melon in half, scoop out the seeds and peel away the skin. Cut the flesh into 72 even-sized pieces.

Fold each piece of prosciutto in half again lengthways and thread on to a cocktail skewer, interweaving with three pieces of melon. Top with a mint leaf. Serve at room temperature.

GARLIC AND HERB STUFFED DATES

We are now lucky enough to find dates on sale right through the winter months. They have a dark golden-brown skin that is slightly wrinkled, encasing a rich, sweet flesh. Makes 24.

450g/1lb fresh dates, 24 in total
100g/4oz low-fat soft cheese
100g/4oz cottage cheese
1 garlic clove, crushed

2 tbsp chopped fresh herbs
freshly ground black pepper
1 tbsp snipped fresh chives

Split the dates along the top and remove the stones and any stalk.

Mix together the low-fat soft cheese and cottage cheese. Beat in the garlic and herbs and season with lots of pepper. Fill each date with the garlic and herb mixture, using a small teaspoon.

Sprinkle the dates with the chives, arrange on a serving plate and cover with cling film. Chill for up to 2 hours before serving.

Right: Niçoise Platter with Garlic Yoghurt

TERIYAKI SALMON WITH HORSERADISH DIP

Salmon escalopes – neat strips of boneless salmon that have been cut across the grain – are sold in most large supermarkets. Serves 4.

6 tbsp light soy sauce	8 x 75g/3oz salmon escalopes, skinned
6 tbsp sweet sherry	1 tbsp white wine vinegar or rice vinegar
1 tbsp soft brown sugar	2 tsp creamed horseradish
2.5cm/1in piece root ginger, crushed	1 tbsp sesame seeds
1 garlic clove, crushed	

Put 4 tablespoons each of the soy sauce and sherry in a small pan with half the sugar, the ginger and garlic and stir over a low heat to dissolve the sugar. Bring to the boil and simmer for about 5 minutes or until reduced and thickened slightly. Leave to cool completely, then strain into a shallow non-metallic dish.

Add the salmon to the soy marinade, turning to coat. Cover and set aside for 30 minutes. Meanwhile, put the remaining soy sauce, sherry and sugar in a small pan with the vinegar and cook over a low heat until the sugar has dissolved. Stir in the horseradish and keep warm.

Preheat the grill. Thread each piece of salmon on to two 15cm/6in bamboo skewers and arrange on a lightly oiled grill rack. Grill for 2 minutes, then turn over and brush with the remaining marinade. Sprinkle evenly with the sesame seeds and grill for another 2–3 minutes or until the salmon is just cooked through. Serve at once, with the horseradish dip.

SWEET AND SOUR VEGETABLE KEBABS

You will find it easier to brush the vegetables with the honey mixture while it is still warm. Any remaining mixture can be served with the kebabs as a dipping sauce. Serves 4.

5 tbsp clear honey	1 red onion, cut into 2.5cm/1in squares
4 tbsp light soy sauce	2 red peppers, seeded and cut into
4 tbsp white wine vinegar	2.5cm/1in squares
2 tsp grated root ginger	8 yellow patty pan squash, halved
1 small red chilli, seeded and	1 tbsp sesame seeds
finely chopped	

Place the honey, soy sauce, vinegar, ginger and chilli in a small pan with 120ml/4floz of water and bring to the boil. Reduce the heat and simmer for 5–10 minutes or until thickened and well reduced.

Preheat the grill. Thread the onion, peppers and patty pan squash on to eight 15cm/6in bamboo skewers. Brush all over with the warm honey mixture and grill for about 15 minutes, turning frequently, until tender and lightly browned. Then sprinkle with the sesame seeds and grill for a further 1–2 minutes or until the seeds are lightly toasted. Serve at once.

CUCUMBER CUPS WITH TARAMASALATA

Cods' roe is the whole roe of the female cod that has been salted, then rinsed and soaked. The outer membrane is then peeled off, leaving the sticky pink roe which is readily available from fishmongers. Makes 24.

6 slices brown bread
1 cucumber, peeled

FOR THE TARAMASALATA

100g/4oz smoked cods' roe, skinned	grated rind and juice of 1 small lemon
1 small garlic clove, crushed	2 tbsp olive oil
25g/1oz fresh white breadcrumbs	freshly ground black pepper
1 small shallot, chopped	

To make the taramasalata, break up the cods' roe, place in a food processor and blend to a purée. Add the garlic, breadcrumbs, shallot, and lemon rind and juice and blend again until smooth. Mix the oil with 3 tablespoons of hot water and pour into the food processor, with the motor running. Season with pepper and chill until ready to use.

Preheat the grill. Using a fluted pastry cutter about the same diameter as the cucumber, cut out 24 circles of bread. Lightly toast them on both sides. Leave to cool on a wire rack.

Cut the cucumber across into 24 slices and remove the seeds, using a teaspoon or an apple corer. Then cut down the sides of each slice with the fluted cutter. Spread each round of toasted bread with a little of the taramasalata. Top with a piece of cucumber and spoon the taramasalata into the centre. Serve at once.

TAPENADE AND TOMATO CROSTINI

Add a little more lemon juice if you find it is needed to bind the olive mixture; no oil is needed. Makes 24.

1 thin French baguette	50g/2oz tuna in brine, drained
1 garlic clove, halved	3 tbsp chopped fresh parsley
100g/4oz pitted black olives	1–2 tbsp lemon juice
2 anchovy fillets in oil, drained, rinsed	salt and freshly ground black pepper
and chopped	225g/8oz small ripe tomatoes, sliced

Preheat the grill. Cut the baguette into 24 slices, discarding the ends. Rub one side of each slice with the halved garlic clove (keep the garlic) and grill for 8–10 minutes, turning once, until golden. Leave to cool on a wire rack.

Place the garlic clove in a food processor with the olives, anchovies, tuna, 1 tablespoon of the parsley and the lemon juice. Blend until fairly smooth. Season to taste.

Spread the toasts with the tapenade and arrange tomato slices on top. Season with pepper, sprinkle over the remaining parsley and serve.

Right: Teriyaki Salmon with Horseradish Dip

BREAD BITES

Sandwiches have become a regular part of our lives, but they need never be boring. So many different breads are now available that it's easy to give a new look to old favourites such as cheese and tomato or salmon and watercress. This chapter goes further, taking inspiration from around the world to come up with some tempting ideas for truly sensational sandwiches. All recipes serve 4.

AUBERGINE AND PESTO GRILLS ON FOCACCIA

This has to be one of the most wonderful vegetarian sandwiches ever. You can make the parcels up to 24 hours in advance, cover them with cling film and chill until ready to grill.

1 large aubergine	*150g/5oz mozzarella cheese*
3 tbsp olive oil	*2 tbsp pesto sauce*
salt and freshly ground black pepper	*1 focaccia loaf*
2 plum tomatoes	*1 garlic clove, halved*

Preheat the grill. Cut the aubergine lengthways into four long slices, discarding the ends. Brush each slice on both sides with a little of the oil, season generously and grill for about 10 minutes, turning occasionally, until softened and lightly golden.

Cut each tomato into four slices, discarding the ends. Cut the mozzarella into four slices. Spread one side of each slice of aubergine with pesto, then arrange two slices of tomato and a slice of mozzarella on top. Bring the sides of the aubergine up around the filling and secure with a wooden cocktail stick.

Cut the foccacia into four pieces and split each one in half horizontally. Brush with the remaining oil and rub with the garlic clove. Grill the aubergine parcels for 3–4 minutes, then add the focaccia and grill for a further 1–2 minutes or until the bread is toasted and the mozzarella has begun to melt. Remove the cocktail sticks from the parcels and sandwich each one between two pieces of focaccia. Serve hot.

CREAMED MUSHROOMS ON BRIOCHE TOASTS

There is now a wide variety of cultivated 'wild' mushrooms available in supermarkets and specialist shops. You can experiment with all sorts of combinations for this dish and get a different result every time.

1 brioche loaf	*1 tbsp brandy*
40g/1½oz butter	*6 tbsp crème fraîche*
350g/12oz mixed wild mushrooms, sliced	*1 tbsp chopped fresh tarragon*
salt and freshly ground black pepper	*1 tbsp chopped fresh flat-leaf parsley*

Cut the brioche loaf into four thick slices, discarding the ends, and set aside. Heat the butter in a frying pan, add the mushrooms and stir-fry for about 5 minutes. Season to taste.

Lightly toast the brioche slices and arrange on serving plates; keep warm. Add the brandy to the mushrooms and then pour in the crème fraîche, stirring. Simmer for a few minutes until thickened, then stir in the tarragon. Spoon the mushroom mixture over the brioche toasts, scatter the parsley on top and serve at once.

PASTRAMI, DILL PICKLE AND MUSTARD MAYO ON SOURDOUGH

Pastrami is the underside or brisket of beef, cured in a mixture of sugar, spices and garlic for about 7 days, then smoked, giving it its characteristic flavour.

1 small round sourdough loaf	*2 tbsp American mustard (from a*
25g/1oz butter, softened	*squeezy bottle)*
12 thin slices pastrami	*2 tbsp mayonnaise*
4 dill pickled cucumbers	*salt and freshly ground black pepper*
	crinkle-cut crisps, to serve

Cut the sourdough loaf into eight slices, discarding the ends, and spread with the butter. Arrange three slices of pastrami on each of four slices of bread, in an overlapping layer. Cut the dill pickle into thin slices and scatter on top.

Mix the mustard with the mayonnaise and season to taste. Thickly spread the remaining slices of bread with the mustard mayonnaise and use to cover the pastrami and dill pickle. Cut the sandwiches in half and serve with crisps.

Above: *Roquefort, Grape and Radicchio on Walnut Bread*

BAGELS WITH SMOKED TROUT RILLETTES

You could use smoked trout trimmings for this recipe, or try using a mixture of fresh and smoked salmon which works just as well. The rillettes can be frozen for up to 1 month. Freeze in a rigid plastic container, and defrost thoroughly before using.

175g/6oz rainbow trout fillet
75ml/3fl oz dry white wine
1 bay leaf
a few black peppercorns
175g/6oz unsalted butter, softened
175g/6oz smoked trout

juice of ¹/2 lemon
good pinch of cayenne pepper
salt and freshly ground black pepper
4 bagels, split
1 tbsp snipped fresh chives

Place the fresh trout in a pan with the wine, bay leaf and peppercorns. Add enough water to cover and simmer for about 5 minutes or until just tender and cooked through. Leave to cool in the liquid.

Melt 50g/2oz of the butter in a frying pan and cook the smoked trout until it turns pale pink. Set aside to cool.

Drain the fresh trout, remove the skin and flake the flesh. Break up the smoked trout and add to the fresh trout. Beat in the remaining butter, the lemon juice, cayenne pepper and seasoning to taste.

Pile the trout rillettes on the bagel halves and sprinkle over the chives.

ROQUEFORT, GRAPE AND RADICCHIO ON WALNUT BREAD

Roquefort is a creamy-white, semi-soft crumbly cheese with greeny/blue marbling. When buying, avoid any with a very white paste or too few veins. It's a good idea to allow the cheese to come up to room temperature before using; this normally takes about an hour.

1 small walnut loaf
25g/1oz butter, softened
275g/10oz Roquefort cheese
1 small head radicchio, shredded

1¹/2 tbsp olive oil
¹/2 tbsp red wine vinegar
salt and freshly ground black pepper
50g/2oz seedless red grapes, halved

Cut the walnut loaf into eight slices, discarding the ends, and lightly butter. Cut any rind off the Roquefort and discard, then cut into thin slices. Arrange the cheese on four slices of bread.

Place the radicchio in a bowl and add the oil, vinegar and seasoning. Toss to coat, then pile on top of the cheese. Scatter over the grapes and cover with the remaining slices of bread. Cut each sandwich in half on the diagonal before serving.

POACHED SALMON AND WATERCRESS MAYONNAISE CRUSTY ROLLS

You can make this mayonnaise in a food processor or blender, but you'll need double the quantity for the machine to work. Put the egg yolks, half the lemon juice and seasoning into the machine and blend for 10 seconds. Then, with the motor running at a low speed, pour in the oil in a thin stream. Stir in the remaining lemon juice with the rind and watercress.

150ml/5floz dry white wine
a few parsley stalks
1 bay leaf
a few black peppercorns
450g/1lb salmon fillet, skinned and boned
1 egg yolk

grated rind and juice of 1 lemon
salt and freshly ground black pepper
75ml/3fl oz sunflower oil
4 tbsp finely chopped watercress
25g/1oz butter, softened
4 large crusty granary rolls, split

Place the wine in a small pan with the parsley, bay leaf and peppercorns. Add the salmon and pour in enough water to cover. Simmer very gently for 5 minutes or until the fish is just cooked through and opaque (don't allow the liquid to boil or the fish will break up). Remove with a fish slice, leave to cool and then break into large flakes.

Place the egg yolk in a bowl with half the lemon juice and seasoning. Whisk thoroughly. Add the oil drop by drop to start with and then in a steady stream, whisking until thickened and smooth. Stir in the watercress, lemon rind and the remaining lemon juice.

Butter the rolls. Pile the salmon flakes on the bottom halves, spoon over the watercress mayonnaise and cover with the tops of the rolls. Serve at once.

CRISPY DUCK WITH MANGO RELISH ON MINI NAAN BREADS

Rubbing salt into the skin of the duckling helps to crisp it, while the honey adds a wonderful sweet-sour flavour. Mini naan breads are now readily available. However, you could also use three ordinary naan breads cut in half.

2 duckling breast fillets, each
about 175g/6oz
1 tsp salt
1 tbsp clear honey
6 mini naan breads
50g/2oz iceberg lettuce, shredded

FOR THE MANGO RELISH
1 mango, peeled and finely chopped
1 green chilli, seeded and finely chopped
1 shallot, finely chopped
juice of 1 lime
1 tsp caster sugar

To make the mango relish, put the mango, chilli, shallot, lime juice and sugar in a small bowl and toss gently to combine. Cover and chill until ready to serve.

Preheat the oven to 180°C/350°F/Gas 4. Prick the duckling breasts all over with a fork and rub well with the salt. Place, skin side up, on a rack in a roasting tin. Roast for 15 minutes, then remove from the oven. Brush the skin with the honey, return to the oven and roast for a further 20 minutes or until cooked through. Leave to rest for 5 minutes, then cut into thin slices.

Arrange the naan breads on a baking tray and sprinkle over a little water. Warm in the oven for 2–3 minutes.

Split each naan in half and arrange three halves on each serving plate. Spread a little of the mango relish on each piece of naan and divide the lettuce among them. Arrange the slices of duck on top in fan shapes and spoon a little more of the relish over each one. Serve with any remaining relish.

HOT KIPPER TOASTS

You could use boil-in-the-bag whole kippers for this recipe, which are normally sold frozen and are a useful standby. Cook according to packet instructions and then continue as below.

350g/12oz kippers
4 tbsp fromage frais
75g/3oz Cheddar cheese, grated

1 tsp Worcestershire sauce
1 ciabatta loaf
1 lemon, cut into wedges

Put the kippers into a large, heatproof jug and pour over enough boiling water to cover. Leave to stand for 5 minutes, then drain. Skin, remove any bones and mash the flesh in a bowl.

Add the fromage frais, Cheddar and Worcestershire sauce. Mix well to combine.

Preheat the grill. Cut the ciabatta into 12 slices on the diagonal, discarding the ends. Lightly toast the ciabatta slices on both sides under the grill, then spread over the kipper mixture and grill until bubbling. Squeeze over a little lemon juice and serve at once.

CURRIED TURKEY WITH APRICOT ON GRANARY

You could use ordinary cooked turkey or chicken for this recipe and still get an excellent result. It's great for using up the leftovers from a Sunday roast and spices up otherwise bland meat.

50g/2oz butter
1 small onion, finely chopped
2 tbsp korma curry paste
150ml/5floz dry white wine
1 tbsp clear honey
8 ready-to-eat dried apricots, finely chopped
4 tbsp mayonnaise

2 tbsp double cream
225g/8oz smoked turkey
8 slices granary bread
50g/2oz iceberg lettuce, shredded
10cm/4in piece cucumber, sliced
4 spring onions, chopped

Melt half the butter in a small pan and gently fry the onion until softened. Add the curry paste, wine, honey and apricots and simmer, uncovered, for 15–20 minutes or until nearly all the liquid is gone. Leave to cool, then stir in the mayonnaise and cream. Remove any skin from the turkey and cut the meat into bite-sized pieces, then fold into the apricot mixture.

Lightly spread the bread with the remaining butter and divide the turkey mixture among four of the slices. Pile the iceberg lettuce on top and scatter over the cucumber and spring onions. Cover with the remaining bread, cut each sandwich in half on the diagonal and serve.

WARM POLENTA AND WILD MUSHROOM SANDWICHES

You could also use quick-cook polenta for these sandwiches. Just follow the instructions on the packet, and stamp out the circles from the prepared slab, as described below.

275g/10oz polenta
salt and freshly ground black pepper
75g/3oz butter
1 garlic clove, crushed
1 tbsp olive oil, plus extra for greasing

2 shallots, sliced
350g/12oz mixed wild mushrooms, sliced
2 tsp lemon juice
2 tbsp chopped fresh parsley

Bring 1.5 litres/2 1/2 pints of cold water to the boil in a large pan. Add 1 teaspoon of salt and pour in the polenta in a continuous thin stream, stirring constantly with a wooden spoon. Simmer for 30 minutes or until the polenta is thickened and no longer grainy, stirring frequently.

Remove the pan from the heat and stir in half the butter and the garlic. Season with pepper. Turn out on to a lightly oiled tray or wooden board and spread out to form a 38 x 25cm/15 x 10in rectangle, about 1cm/1/2in thick. Leave to cool, then cover and chill for at least 1 hour.

Preheat the grill. Using a 7.5cm/3in round cutter, stamp out eight rounds from the set polenta. Brush them lightly with oil and place on a foil-lined grill pan. Grill for 3–4 minutes on each side. Cover loosely and keep warm.

Heat the remaining butter in a large frying pan and sauté the shallots for 2 minutes. Add the mushrooms and sauté for a further 3–4 minutes. Sprinkle over the lemon juice and parsley and stir to mix.

Arrange four of the polenta rounds on warmed serving plates and divide the mushroom mixture among them. Place the remaining rounds on top and serve.

LOIN OF PORK, BEETROOT AND HORSERADISH ON LIGHT RYE

These sandwiches are at their best when the pork is still warm. Don't try to make them in advance as the beetroot will run and discolour the meat and bread.

675g/1 1/2 lb loin of pork
2 tsp chopped fresh rosemary
2 tbsp Dijon mustard
2 tbsp lemon juice
4 tbsp clear honey

25g/1oz butter, softened
8 slices light rye bread
2 tbsp creamed horseradish
2 cooked beetroots, thinly sliced

Preheat the oven to 200°C/400°F/Gas 6. Remove the chine bone (backbone) from the pork loin and cut off the rib bones, or ask your butcher to do this for you. Place the pork loin in a small roasting tin and roast for 30 minutes.

Mix together the rosemary, mustard, lemon juice and honey. Remove the pork from the oven and brush all over with the rosemary and mustard glaze. Return to the oven to roast for a further 15 minutes, basting occasionally with the glaze, until well browned and tender. Leave to rest for 15 minutes before carving into slices.

Lightly butter the bread and smear with the horseradish. Arrange the slices of pork on four of the slices and top with the beetroot. Cover with the remaining bread and cut in half on the diagonal to serve.

SUN-DRIED TOMATO, AVOCADO AND MOZZARELLA ON FOCACCIA

This variation on the classic is very good for the winter months when fresh tomatoes have lost their intense flavour, but good mozzarella and avocados are still available.

12 sun-dried tomatoes preserved in oil, drained and oil reserved
4 tbsp pesto sauce
2 tsp lemon juice

1 focaccia loaf
275g/10oz mozzarella cheese, thinly sliced
1 large avocado, sliced
freshly ground black pepper

Cut the drained tomatoes into slivers. Place the reserved oil from the tomatoes in a bowl and stir in the pesto and lemon juice until thoroughly mixed. Cut the focaccia in half horizontally and spread the pesto mixture on the cut surfaces.

Arrange the mozzarella on one piece of focaccia and scatter over the tomato slivers. Put the avocado slices on top and season with plenty of pepper. Sandwich the focaccia back together and press down lightly. Cut into four equal pieces and serve.

Right: Sun-Dried Tomato, Avocado and Mozzarella on Focaccia

ALL-AMERICAN CLUB SANDWICH

The club sandwich is a classic American restaurant speciality that has lasted the test of time. There are numerous variations, and you can create your own combination, depending on the contents of the fridge!

1 tbsp wholegrain mustard	25g/1oz iceberg lettuce, finely shredded
6 tbsp mayonnaise	2 tomatoes, sliced
salt and freshly ground black pepper	1 small white salad onion, cut into
8 smoked streaky bacon rashers	wafer-thin slices
8 slices white bread	100g/4oz wafer-thin chicken slices
4 slices brown bread	4 thin slices of Gruyère cheese

Mix the mustard, mayonnaise and seasoning in a small bowl. Preheat the grill and grill the bacon until crisp; crumble coarsely or chop it. Lightly toast all the bread, then spread with the mustard mayonnaise.

Divide half the lettuce among four slices of white bread, top with the tomato and half the onion slices and season to taste. Cover with the chicken and place the brown bread slices on top, mayonnaise side up.

Pile the remaining lettuce on the slices of brown bread and place the cheese on top. Scatter over the bacon and the remaining onion. Cover with the remaining white bread slices, mayonnaise side down, and press down lightly. Cut each sandwich into four triangles and secure each piece with a cocktail stick or small plastic skewer. Serve at once.

ROAST BEEF AND ROCKET ON RYE WITH MUSTARD DRESSING

Use the tip of a small sharp knife to make the incisions in the beef for the garlic slivers. The rich flavour of rye bread, sometimes called black bread, is the perfect accompaniment for beef.

350g/12oz fillet of beef	1 tbsp white wine vinegar
1 large garlic clove, cut into slivers	2 tsp Dijon mustard
salt and freshly ground black pepper	75g/3oz tender young rocket leaves
4 tbsp sunflower oil	25g/1oz butter, softened
1 tbsp walnut oil	8 slices rye bread

Preheat the oven to 230°C/450°F/Gas 8. Bring the beef fillet to room temperature, stud with the slivers of garlic and season well all over. Heat 2 tablespoons of the sunflower oil in a small frying pan until very hot and fry the beef for 1 minute on each side to seal.

Transfer the beef to a small roasting tin and roast for 20 minutes. Remove from the oven and leave to rest for 10 minutes before carving into thin slices, discarding the slivers of garlic.

To make the dressing, place the remaining sunflower oil, the walnut oil, vinegar, mustard and seasoning in a screw-topped jar and shake well. Place the rocket in a bowl, add the dressing and toss to coat.

Lightly butter the rye bread and divide the slices of beef among four of them. Pile on the dressed rocket and top with the remaining bread. Cut each sandwich in half on the diagonal and serve.

MUFFULETTA

This is one of the most impressive sandwiches you are ever likely to see. It is based on a recipe from way down south in the USA, and is perfect for picnics (as it transports beautifully) or as part of a buffet. Serves 8–10.

2 small aubergines, cut into slices lengthways	6 tbsp pesto sauce
4 small courgettes, cut into slices lengthways	100g/4oz sun-dried tomatoes preserved in oil, drained
olive oil, for brushing	400g/14oz buffalo mozzarella, thinly sliced
2 yellow peppers, seeded and quartered	225g/8oz garlic salami, thinly sliced and rind removed
1 round country bread, such as pugliese	175g/6oz tender young spinach leaves
1 garlic clove, halved	salt and freshly ground black pepper

Preheat the grill. Brush the aubergine and courgette slices with oil and arrange on a grill rack with the peppers. Grill for 8–10 minutes, turning the aubergine and courgette slices occasionally, until cooked through and lightly browned. When the pepper skins are blackened and blistered, wrap in cling film and leave to cool, with the other vegetables. When cool, peel off the pepper skins.

Cut a lid off the top of the loaf, then hollow out the middle, leaving a shell about 2.5cm/1in thick. Rub the inside of the bread shell all over with the garlic and then spread with the pesto.

Arrange the aubergine slices in an overlapping layer on the bottom of the shell and scatter the sun-dried tomatoes on top. Add the courgettes, followed by the mozzarella, then the salami and finally the peppers. Season each layer generously as you go. Finish with the spinach, and replace the top of the loaf. Wrap tightly in cling film and chill overnight, pressed down by a heavy weight. Unwrap the muffuletta, cut into thick wedges and serve.

CROQUE MONSIEUR CROISSANTS

You could use the chilled croissant dough which is now available in cylinder form at most major supermarkets. Follow the instructions on the packet, placing the filling in the centre of each croissant. Add an extra 15 minutes to the baking time stated on the packet.

4 fresh croissants	150g/5oz Gruyère cheese, grated
1 tbsp Dijon mustard	freshly ground black pepper
4 thin slices roast ham, cut into strips	25g/1oz butter, cut into pieces

Preheat the grill. Split each croissant in half horizontally, not cutting all the way through. Spread Dijon mustard thinly over the open croissants and scatter over the ham. Sprinkle each croissant with 25g/1oz Gruyère. Season with pepper.

Grill the open croissants for 2–3 minutes or until the cheese is bubbling and melted. Then close up each croissant and sprinkle over the remaining cheese. Dot with the butter and grill for a further 1–2 minutes. Serve at once.

Right: Muffuletta

EGG AND BACON MUFFINS WITH PAN-FRIED TOMATOES

These are the perfect late-night snack or early morning 'cure', depending on what the doctor ordered! You don't have to use the metal cutters, just let the fried eggs drape over the top of the muffins.

2 large ripe tomatoes	*4 eggs*
2 tsp seasoned flour	*2 English muffins, split*
4 tbsp sunflower oil	*25g/1oz butter, softened*
8 smoked back bacon rashers	*salt and freshly ground black pepper*

Cut each tomato into six slices, discarding the ends. Place the seasoned flour on a plate and dip in the tomato slices to coat lightly. Heat half the oil in a large frying pan and fry the tomato slices for about 1 minute on each side. Remove from the pan and keep warm.

Preheat the grill and grill the bacon until cooked through. Keep hot.

Place four 7.5cm/3in metal cutters in the frying pan with the remaining oil and heat until very hot. Break an egg into each cutter and cook for 2–3 minutes, spooning the oil over the yolks until the eggs are just set.

Meanwhile, lightly toast the muffins and spread with the butter. Place two bacon rashers on each muffin half and arrange three slices of pan-fried tomato in an overlapping layer on top. Remove the frying pan from the heat and carefully lift out the metal cutters. Top each muffin with an egg, season to taste and serve at once.

MARINATED STEAK BAGUETTES

This recipe produces a medium-rare steak, but you can adjust the cooking times to suit personal preferences. Grill for 2 minutes on each side for a rare steak and 6–7 minutes on each side for it to be cooked right through.

4 x 100g/4oz sirloin steaks, about 2cm/3/4in thick	*1 tsp fresh thyme leaves*
salt and freshly ground black pepper	*4 x 10cm/4in pieces French baguette, split*
3 tbsp olive oil	*2 tbsp Dijon mustard*
1 tbsp red wine vinegar	*40g/1 1/2oz frisée lettuce, torn into small pieces*
1 large garlic clove, crushed	

Trim the steaks of all fat, season well and place in a non-metallic dish. Mix together the olive oil, red wine vinegar, garlic and thyme in a small bowl and spoon over the steaks, turning to coat. Cover and leave in the fridge to marinate for at least 30 minutes and up to 24 hours.

Preheat the grill. Shake the steaks to remove any excess marinade and grill for 3–4 minutes on each side. Lightly toast the baguette.

Spread the mustard on the cut sides of the baguette, then sandwich a steak and some lettuce between two pieces. Serve at once.

PEPERONATA WITH GOAT'S CHEESE CIABATTA

The colourful, spicy sweetness of the peppers and the creaminess of the goat's cheese make an outstanding combination.

4 tbsp chilli oil	*1 large garlic clove, crushed*
1 red and 1 yellow pepper, seeded and thinly sliced	*75g/3oz round goat's cheese*
2 tsp cumin seeds	*1 ciabatta loaf*
salt and freshly ground black pepper	*1 tbsp chopped fresh parsley*

Heat the oil in a large heavy-based frying pan, add the peppers and cumin seeds and fry over a high heat for 2–3 minutes. Season generously, then reduce the heat and stir in the garlic. Cook for a further 10 minutes, stirring occasionally, until the peppers have caramelised around the edges. Leave to cool slightly.

Cut the goat's cheese into four slices. Cut the ciabatta in half horizontally and then across to make four pieces. Spread the peperonata on the cut surfaces of the ciabatta and place a slice of goat's cheese on top. Sprinkle over the parsley and serve.

SAUSAGE TORPEDOES WITH CARAMELISED ONIONS

This is a real kid's favourite and is great served with chips. You could also cook the sausages on the barbecue for the same length of time.

4 good-quality pork sausages	*FOR THE BARBECUE SAUCE*
1 onion, cut into thick slices	*6 tbsp tomato ketchup*
1 tbsp seasoned flour	*1 tbsp each soy sauce and lemon juice*
2 tbsp sunflower oil	*1 tsp each Dijon mustard and clear honey*
4 long crusty white bread rolls	
25g/1oz iceberg lettuce, shredded	

To make the barbecue sauce, mix all the ingredients in a small bowl.

Preheat the grill. Place the sausages in a small non-metallic baking dish. Pour over half the barbecue sauce and spread it evenly all over the sausages. Grill the sausages for 10–15 minutes, turning and basting occasionally with any sauce left in the dish.

Meanwhile, separate the onion into rings and dust with the seasoned flour. Heat the oil in a frying pan and stir-fry the onion rings until crisp and golden. Remove with a slotted spoon and drain on kitchen paper.

Split the rolls lengthways and fill them with the lettuce. Lay the sausages on top and drizzle over the remaining barbecue sauce. Scatter over the onion rings and serve hot.

Right: Peperonata with Goat's Cheese Ciabatta

RECIPE INDEX

First published in 1996 by

George Weidenfeld & Nicolson Limited

The Orion Publishing Group

Orion House

5 Upper St. Martin's Lane

London WC2H 9EA

British Library Cataloguing -in-Publication Data

A catalogue record for this book is available
from the British Library.

ISBN 0-2972-83580-7

Designed by The Design Revolution, Brighton

Editor: Laura Washburn

Stylist: Roisin Nield

Home Economist: Carol Tennant